TENACIOUS
LOVE

A Journey with Jesus in Choosing to Love Others

VALERIE JAMESON

Trilogy Christian Publishers
A Wholly Owned Subsidiary of Trinity Broadcasting Network
2442 Michelle Drive
Tustin, CA 92780

For information, address Trilogy Christian Publishing
Rights Department, 2442 Michelle Drive, Tustin, Ca 92780.
Trilogy Christian Publishing/ TBN and colophon are trademarks of Trinity Broadcasting Network.

For information about special discounts for bulk purchases, please contact Trilogy Christian Publishing.

Manufactured in the United States of America

10 9 8 7 6 5 4 3 2 1

Library of Congress Cataloging-in-Publication Data is available.

ISBN 978-1-64773-997-3 (Print Book)
ISBN 978-1-64773-998-0 (ebook)

Living in the awareness of the Lord's tenacious love for us and seeking Him for His power to love tenaciously through us is so liberating to our heart and soul. Christ came to set us free and this book shows how to practically board this freedom train for the soul.

L. Spangler

I loved this book and gained such life-changing insight that has led me to victory by allowing the Holy Spirit to redirect my thoughts that then lead to actions when faced with rejection, betrayal, and pain from those I have trusted. It is necessary to recognize the lens we have formerly looked through and allow Him to give us new vision based on truth and not past encounters.

R. Burns

Why does God love us? How can He love us? This book is a powerful testimony of God's great love. An engaging and powerful read.

C. Nelson

I have been overwhelmed and in awe of God's tenacious love for me as He calls me to love like Him.

M. Karkkainen

This book is dedicated to my Savior and best friend, Jesus Christ, who has loved me tenaciously my entire life and has given me the most amazing journey a girl could ever ask for. And to my amazing husband, Kevin, who has faithfully stood beside me through it all. I love you.

CONTENTS

FOREWORD

I remember the first time I met Valerie Jameson. It was an unforgettable moment. I was working as a juvenile probation officer when she came to my office with a group of excited young ladies. They were her soccer team and she was their coach. They brought good tidings of joy and lots of food for the Thanksgiving holiday to feed several of my needy families. It was a sight to behold. But I was most struck with Valerie's infectious energy and enthusiasm that to this day remains unmatched in any of my other friendships. It was no surprise that we became fast friends, but what connected us the most was and still is our love for Jesus.

Through the years I have had the opportunity to watch Valerie's love for Jesus manifest itself in love for others. As I write this, I am certain she would not want me to have shared this with you because she lives with a precious and authentic quality of humility. This stems from a powerful yearning to turn attention away from herself and instead turn attention to her Lord and Savior. She desires nothing less than glorifying God in words and deeds. Be this as it may, I have been changed by watching her take the journey of the Christian faith. Valerie has come to describe her walk of faith as a journey of "tenacious" love. I believe she has received meaningful insight as to how God loves us tenaciously, and then asks and enables us to love others this way. Through her own personal experiences and the experiences of others, her writings are meant to showcase tenacious love so that we can understand this love at the deepest possible spiritual level.

More than ever, this book is needed in our world today because tenacious love can stir the hearts of humanity. Though I dare to warn you, loving tenaciously will not be easy. You will be challenged to say and do things that you never thought possible. But if you persevere and practice, practice, practice, the benefits will be experienced not only in this present life but for all eternity.

To conclude, in my own journey to love tenaciously, I can't help but turn to the greatest love story ever told in the Bible. It took place in a garden, the Garden of Gethsemane. Simply put, Jesus was about to lose His life in a most horrific and unimaginable way, so that we could find ours. I refer to this time as a "garden moment," and you and I face them all the time. It is these moments where we can feel betrayed, disappointed, hurt, lonely, falsely accused, unforgiven, or unloved. And yet, whether life is about our Lord tenaciously loving us or it is the opportunity for us to love others this way, tenacious love will always be the answer. So read on, my friends, and may you be encouraged to start a new journey of loving others in a way that will bless you beyond measure. And know that after every "garden moment" is a resurrection!

Sherry Anderson

INTRODUCTION

"Lord, who am I? Why am I here? What do You want me to do? To be?"

That is where it all started, with me asking God the big questions. And guess what? He answered me, as only He does. In the quietness of my spirit, He answered. I know this may sound strange to some, but I am here to tell you that God does truly speak in ways that may not be audible but are just as powerful! You see, God placed it on my heart to write down four questions: *Who am I? Where am I going? What's my platform?* and *What do I stand for?* Then He showed me the answers: You are My child, a daughter of the King; you go where I send you. Your platform is your life, and you stand for love.

Little did I know that those beautiful words from my heavenly Father over ten years ago would shape my existence, my life, my everything. As I continued to pursue Him more and more throughout the years, I found all I wanted to do was to love Him and bring Him glory. The world around me started to fade as I focused on those four powerful focal points that He gave me. As each new year arrived, I would find myself wanting to do more and more for Him. I would go to Him and ask if there was anything else, any other message. Perhaps a new focal word of the year? You see, my sister would receive new words from Him every year, and every year my word would remain the same...LOVE. I have to admit that I may have been a bit bummed when my sister would reveal her new word each year and mine would remain the same. Don't get me wrong, love is a big one...a really big one. I just didn't quite realize how big until He led me to the next part of my journey. My focus up until that point was to love Him and others the best I could, but somehow I still had a stirring and a desire to do more.

Until one morning when I was sitting in a hotel room during a trip. I asked Him, "Lord, there is so much brokenness in this world. What more can I do? I want to glorify You by using my life to make a difference. I know You want me to love, but how?" It was then, once again in the quietness of my spirit, that He answered me. He whispered, "Tenaciously." Knowing that I am a visual girl, He had me write down something. "Write the capital letter *L* for love and the capital letter *T* for tenacious and put them together. What do you get?"

When I did, I was blown away...it was the CROSS! I have to admit, I was shaken to the point of tears. "Thank You, God, for giving me this beautiful visual reminder of what tenacious love is. It isn't about me *at all*, it is about Jesus, *the* tenacious Lover of all mankind!"

My "how" question led me to the greatest yet most challenging journey I have ever been on. You see, up until this point I was trying to love in my own strength, trying to muster up what I thought I was supposed to do. I made everything about myself and I had no clue of what it meant to truly love tenaciously. But that was not what God wanted from me. He wanted me to look to *Jesus* as my example, submit to the power of the Holy Spirit, and learn to intentionally *choose* to love tenaciously, no matter the circumstances, just as He did. I want to make very clear that this is not a faith that comes from a work type of study, it is a relationship journey with our precious Jesus.

My desire for all who read this book is to help you begin the same beautiful tenacious love journey with Jesus that I am on, just you and Him. I am not anything special, just a foolish vessel Jesus blessed with a divine message that is meant to be shared. After all, each one of us has been created in His image and He has a special message and calling for each one of us for such a time as this. Let the tenacious love journey begin!

Prayer:

Lord, You have created me for a special purpose for such a time as this. As I embark on this tenacious love journey, please prepare my heart for what You would like to teach me.

This journal is your safe place. This is only between you and God.

Reflection:

- *Do you feel a stirring from God calling you to love Him and others more? If so, journal what God is calling you to do.*

Journal:

_____

_____

_____

_____

_____

PART ONE

TENACIOUS LOVE

According to Oxford English Dictionary, the word tenacious can be defined as "tending to keep a firm hold of something, clinging or adhering closely, determined and not readily relinquishing a position or principle or course of action, and persisting in existence; not easily dispelled."

When looking at our English word for love, you will find definitions such as an intense feeling of deep affection and a strong feeling of affection and sexual attraction for someone. This, my friends, is how we as a society have viewed love: driven by emotions. However, we are going to hone in on a different kind of love, *tenacious love*, the kind that Jesus called us to. "A new commandment I give to you, that you *love* one another; as I have loved you, that you also *love* one another" (John 13:34 NKJV, emphasis added).

This is a different kind of love, one that is powered not by emotion but by *choice*. The Greek word for this kind of love is *agape*. It speaks of a motivation for action. This type of love is a sacrificial love that one voluntarily chooses. It's inconvenient, uncomfortable, and selfless. Jesus called us, as His followers, to love each other with this kind of love, because that is the very love that He demonstrates for each of us.

"Therefore, if you have any encouragement from being united with Christ, if any comfort from His love, if any common sharing in the Spirit, if any tenderness and compassion, then make my joy complete by being like-minded, having the same love, being one in spirit and of one mind. Do nothing out of selfish ambition or vain conceit. Rather, in humility value others above yourselves, not looking to your own interests but each of you to the interests of others.

"In your relationships with one another, have the same mindset as Jesus Christ: who being in very nature God, did not consider equality with God something to be used to His own advantage; rather, he made himself nothing by taking the very nature of a servant, being made in human likeness. And being found in appearance as a man, He humbled Himself by becoming obedient to death—even death on a cross!

"Therefore God exalted him to the highest place and gave him the name that is above every name, that at the name of Jesus every knee should bow, in heaven and on earth and under the earth, and every tongue acknowledge that Jesus Christ is Lord, to the glory of God the Father" (Philippians 2:1–11 NIV).

Reflection:

- *Read the synonyms for tenacious below and think about your life.*

Resolute · Unfaltering · Determined · Faithful· Devoted · Indomitable

Steadfast · Resolute · Constant · Relentless

- *What are you tenaciously holding on to? What drives you?*

(If you need help, think about what you spend most of your time doing, what occupies your thoughts, and where you spend most of your money.)

Journal:

Merriam-Webster. (n.d.). Love. In English. Retrieved June 18, 2017, from https://www.merriam-webster.com/dictionary/love

Oxford Dictionary. (n.d). Tenacious. In Oxford. Retrieved June 18, 2017, from https://www.oed.com/

CHAPTER ONE

The Tenacious One

Have you ever considered what Jesus sacrificed in order to show us love? I am talking *true love*. I am completely overwhelmed when I consider the full scope of His sacrifice for mankind. He left the comforts and royal position of heaven to be born in the lowliest of conditions to a young teenage girl, to persist in His existence, to die on a Roman cross…all in order to begin the greatest journey in history. And all of this with you and me on His mind.

As Oswald Chambers so eloquently put it in his book *My Utmost for His Highest*, "He gave Himself for us—totally, unconditionally, and without reservation." The question is why? Why did He choose to do this for humanity, for those who would mock Him, slander Him, beat Him, and murder Him? For us? While the answer may seem simple, it is the greatest of all gifts. It is because of His tenacious love for His creation.

Jesus humbled Himself, chose to be simple in appearance, was held in low esteem, rejected, misunderstood, afflicted, and oppressed, yet He did not open His mouth. He was unfairly judged yet took the brunt of all mankind's sin and *chose* to forgive, be patient, be compassionate, be selfless, be others focused, be sacrificial, and be self-controlled.

There is no other throughout history that I would rather follow that God's own Son, Jesus Christ. Because He chose to wrap Himself in human flesh, He experienced everything you and I face while living in this world, yet He chose to respond in a way that always brought honor to His Father. All this so we could have the perfect example of how to love tenaciously.

When we look at why Jesus came through the lens of His tenacious love, we will never be the same. He has called each of us to follow His example to love one another, through the power of the Holy Spirit. This journey will *not* be easy, as it requires each of us to put ourselves aside and look to Him to help us love others unconditionally and sacrificially. This journey will test you to the greatest extremes; however, through the power of the Holy Spirit, I believe you will experience a freedom from emotions that up until now have led you astray. You know those hidden emotions that no one sees but God. Those thoughts, those frustrations, those insecurities, that hidden anger and the bitterness that are the result of hurts, jealousy, and straight-up dislikes that come with living in this world…aka people.

Jesus, as God, chose to become human. Through the incarnation, meaning "flesh" in Latin, the divine and humanity became one in the person of Jesus Christ. Because of Adam and Eve's choice in the garden to disobey God, sin entered the world and the broken sinful state of mankind became every individual's plight. God loved His creation and instituted the concept of substitutionary sacrifice through the sacrifice of animals as a way for humanity to acknowledge their sins before Him. However, these animals, while they may have been without spot or blemish on the outside, could not take away sin; a perfect sacrifice had to be made on behalf of mankind. That perfect sacrifice came in the person of Jesus Christ. "For God so loved the world that he gave his one and only Son, that whoever believes in Him shall not perish but have eternal life" (John 3:16 NIV).

Because Jesus chose to love humanity tenaciously by redeeming each one through His sacrifice on the cross, all who choose to believe in Him shall not perish but have everlasting life.

While Jesus' gift does not require us to work for it, it does require a choice. Just as Jesus chose to lay down His own life for you and me, we, my friend, must choose to surrender to His Lordship over our lives. In order to truly have the power to love tenaciously, we must receive God's tenacious love for us. Because we have a Savior, Jesus Christ, who sympathizes and empathizes with us and has experienced every emotion that we as humanity face, we can trust Him and look to Him as our perfect example of how to love tenaciously as well. The first step is knowing how much He loves you. Do you know that before the foundations of the earth were formed, He had you in mind? (See Ephesians 1:4–5.)

Do you know that He built you uniquely and knit you together in your mother's womb for such a time as this? (See Psalm 139:13.) While the world may make you feel like you don't matter, the truth is that you were built by the Master Creator for a purpose...a very special calling that only *you* were created for. Through God's tenacious love, *every* person is valued and loved by Him. If you have sinned and feel that you are not worthy of such love, well, my friend, you are not alone. I too have lived in this place of defeat and know how hopeless it can feel. However, if we are going to take on the emotions that lead us down a path of despair, then this one is at the top of the list. I have great news for you: You don't have to stay in this place. There *is* hope through the redeeming blood of the One who loves you more than anyone, Jesus Christ. The truth is that Jesus loves you, period. You don't have to try to clean yourself up to be "good enough." In actuality, my friend, none of us are ever good enough. He just wants you to come as you are, dirt, stains, grime…bring it all to Him. After all, that is why He came and why He chose to put Himself on the cross. Just come…

"When the scribes and Pharisees saw Him eating with the tax collectors and sinners, they said to His disciples, 'How is it that He eats and drinks with tax collectors and sinners?' When Jesus heard it, He said to them, 'Those who are well have no need of a physician, but those who are sick. I did not come to call the righteous, but sinners, to repentance'" (Mark 2:16–17 NKJV).

If you have never asked Jesus to be your Lord and Savior, or perhaps have strayed and become lukewarm in your relationship with Him and desire to start afresh, then today is your day. *This* is your divine moment. He is calling you. What will you choose?

Romans 10:9 (NIV) states that "if you declare with your mouth, 'Jesus is Lord,' and believe in your heart that God raised him from the dead, you will be saved. For it is with your heart that you believe and are justified, and it is with your mouth that you profess your faith and are saved."

If you have chosen to start a new life right now by receiving Jesus as your personal Savior, then I encourage you to pray this prayer:

Lord, I choose You! I acknowledge that I am a sinner and have made choices that have separated me from You. Lord, I confess that I am broken and need You. I have tried to do things in my own strength and cannot do it. I believe that You died for me on the cross and rose from the grave three days later, and through Your cleansing blood, I am made new. My sins have now been washed away, because of Your choice to give Your life as a ransom for mine. Thank You, Jesus. I receive Your cleansing blood over my life and ask that You protect me, guide me, grant me wisdom, and help me live a life that brings You honor. Please fill me with Your Holy Spirit that I may have the power to follow Your example and love You and others with the same tenacious love. Thank You, precious Jesus! I love You. Amen!

Congratulations, you have just made the most important decision of your entire life! Do you hear that? The celebration in heaven? The Bible tells us in Luke 15:10 that there is joy in the presence of God's angels over one sinner who repents. Yes, they are having a party in heaven right now for *you*! Welcome to the family, dear one!

So, put your seatbelt on, dear friend, and let's jump into this journey together! With the Lord's help, this is the beginning of something huge, and the best part of it is that we get to bless the heart of God by our intentional choice to love Him and others tenaciously!

Now, let the tenacious love journey begin…

Reflection:

- *Who is Jesus, the tenacious One, to you?*

- *How does knowing what Jesus went through for you make you feel?*

- *What do you believe He is calling you to choose?*

Journal:

_____
_____
_____
_____
_____
_____
_____
_____
_____
_____
_____
_____
_____
_____
_____
_____
_____
_____
_____
_____
_____
_____
_____
_____
_____
_____
_____
_____

CHAPTER TWO

The Choice

Now that you have received Jesus as your personal Savior and have the power of the Holy Spirit within you, get ready to battle. You now have an enemy that would like to see you fail. Do not be afraid, but be aware. First Peter 5:8 mentions this enemy, the devil, and says he is like a roaring lion, looking for someone to devour. However, God tells us in 1 John 4:4 that greater is He, the Holy Spirit, who is in you than he who is in the world...aka the enemy.

Let's put things into proper perspective. The enemy is a created being; *you*, however, now belong to the Creator. He has your back, but keep this in mind: you still must be intentional regarding your choices. This, my friend, is where the rubber meets the road. *Daily choices.*

"Submit yourselves, then, to God. Resist the devil, and he will flee from you. Come near to God and he will come near to you" (James 4:7–8 NIV).

I do not like talking about the enemy, because I would rather use my breath to talk about my Savior. But I also think it's important to know who we are dealing with. The enemy comes to lie, kill, and destroy. Period. When we have been hurt, offended, or angered, we stew. We "replay" the hurt over and over again until it gives birth to resentment. What fills our minds fills our hearts and usually spills out in how we treat others. "Each tree is recognized by its own fruit. People do not pick figs from thornbushes, or grapes from briars. A good man brings good things out of the good stored up in his heart, and an evil man brings evil things out of the evil stored up in his heart. For the mouth speaks what the heart is full of" (Luke 6:44–45 NIV).

The enemy can use our encounters with others—through words, actions, or oftentimes silence—to play on our insecurities...*if* we allow him to. He knows our buttons and boy, does he like to push them. What happens when we allow negative thoughts to fester? Well, I can tell you firsthand that the enemy will twist and manipulate your thoughts until you wholeheartedly believe what that person did or said to hurt or offend you was 100 percent personal and that you need to defend or retaliate in some way in order to keep your pride. In reality, when we filter these thoughts through the truth of God's Word, we find that we have a *choice* in how we respond. If we look to Jesus as our example and surrender to the power of the Holy Spirit, then, and only then, can we choose to replace those thoughts with God-honoring thoughts, result-ing in God-honoring choices, resulting in His tenacious love being manifested in and through us.

Colossians 3:1–10 (NIV) tells us, "Since, then, you have been raised with Christ, *set* your hearts on things above, where Christ is, seated at the right hand of God. Set your minds on things above, not on earthly things. For you died, and your life is now hidden with Christ in God. When Christ, who is your life, appears, then you also will appear with Him in glory." We are called, as new creations, to "put to death, therefore, whatever belongs to our earthly nature:

sexual immorality, impurity, lust, evil desires and greed, which is idolatry. Because of these, the wrath of God is coming. You used to walk in these ways, in the life you once lived. *But now* you must also *rid* yourselves of all such things as these: rage, malice, slander, and filthy language from your lips. Do not lie to each other, since you have taken off your old self with its practices and have put on the new self, which is being renewed in knowledge in the *image* of its Creator" (emphasis added).

If you have not yet noticed a theme, I imagine it's starting to ring clear. *Choice.*

We are called to *set* our minds on things that are honoring to God.

Philippians 4:8 (NIV) encourages us in this: "Whatever is true, whatever is noble, whatever is right, whatever is pure, whatever is lovely, whatever is admirable—if anything is excellent or praiseworthy, think about such things."

We are called to *rid* ourselves of rage, malice, slander, and filthy language.

As an athlete and a former coach, I like tactics. One of my favorite phrases is "Offense wins games, but defense wins championships." It's important that we have a plan, because emotions will always be there and so will the enemy, trying to use them to stumble us. While I truly believe that we can never be taken from God after we have received Him as our Lord and Savior, I do believe the enemy can try to snare us, and he often does this through our own emotions. However, we have the power of the Holy Spirit living in us—yes, the same power that raised Christ from the grave! So with that being said, let's win this championship called life! And let's do it together!

Why are tactics so important? If you don't have a defense, then you are at the mercy of the "attacker."

Let's face it, we cannot love others when we are so wrapped up in our own junk. What would happen if we dared to say "Stop, Pray, Filter" (SPF)?

STOP the "brain train" from taking you to a place that you don't want to go. *Choose* what you will do. How can you honor God by loving the very ones who have offended you?

PRAY and ask the Holy Spirit to redirect your thoughts.

FILTER your emotions through God's Word and Jesus' example and allow the Holy Spirit to reveal the truth and the plan of action.

Remember, we must take offenses to God immediately and ask Him to replace the thoughts that may lead to fleshly responses with thoughts that honor Him. We must also remember that the "offender" is not the enemy. Satan is the enemy and it's he who is pulling the strings. "For though we walk in the flesh, we do not war according to the flesh. For the weapons of our warfare are not carnal but mighty in God for pulling down strongholds, casting down arguments and every high thing that exalts itself against the knowledge of God, bringing every thought into captivity to the obedience of Christ" (2 Corinthians 10:3–5 NKJV).

Why is it so important to be disciplined in our thought life? Because that, my friend, is where the battles are won or lost. If we ask the Holy Spirit to teach us to discipline our thought life, then we can have control over the emotions that tend to lead us astray, resulting in loving God and others tenaciously.

Journal:

_____

_____

_____

_____

_____

_____

_____

_____

_____

_____

_____

_____

_____

_____

_____

_____

_____

_____

_____

_____

_____

_____

_____

_____

_____

_____

PART TWO

THE POWER

As followers of Jesus Christ, we have been gifted with the Holy Spirit. The person of the Holy Spirit was given to believers to help teach, instruct, guide, convict, and counsel each of us through this life. As stated in Galatians 5:22, His presence in our lives will be revealed through the fruit of the Spirit: love, joy, peace, patience, kindness, goodness, faithfulness, gentleness, and self-control. It is evident as we look around at the world and take a realistic look at our own fallen human nature that we can only love tenaciously through the power of the Holy Spirit. This begins with our thought life, and taking captive every thought.

Romans 8:5–9 (NIV) tells us that "those who live according to the flesh have their minds set on what the flesh desires; but those who live in accordance with the Spirit have their minds set on what the Spirit desires. The mind governed by the flesh is death, but the mind governed by the Spirit is life and peace. The mind governed by the flesh is hostile to God; it does not submit to God's law, nor can it do so. Those who are in the realm of the flesh cannot please God. You, however, are not in the realm of the flesh but are in the realm of the Spirit; if indeed the Spirit of God lives in you."

I believe we can have the best intentions of living a life that pleases God, but slowly, over time, we can become so busy with our lives that next thing we know, we find ourselves reacting to others instead of responding. I cannot emphasize how important it is to stay "plugged into the power" of the Holy Spirit daily!

My husband and I own a large vehicle that has two batteries and really is a beast of a vehicle...when it starts. When the weather gets a little chilly we have to be intentional about plugging it in to a power source so it will have enough power to start in inclement weather. The other day, we forgot to plug it in. We were busy doing other things and just forgot. When we went to start it, being a diesel, it spewed the blackest, grossest exhaust and sounded like Chitty-Chitty-Bang-Bang. It then hit me: I am like this vehicle! When I am plugged into God's Word and I ask the Holy Spirit to power me up for the day, then I am able to run and accomplish anything God puts in front of me. However, when I forget to plug in or don't think I need to plug in, then I emit the darkest, grossest attitude and I don't run well because I am running on flesh power, not Spirit power. And now instead of loving others tenaciously, I become an offense, I become the offender because my heart is of flesh and not spirit. That is when I hurt others and become a stumbling block.

We must remember, friend, that submitting to the Holy Spirit is a daily choice. What we "feed" on will end up powering us. The Bible speaks of the acts of the flesh in contrast to the fruit of the Spirit. The acts of the flesh include sexual immorality, impurity, idolatry, hatred, discord, jealousy, fits of rage, selfish ambition, dissections, factions, envy, and drunkenness. While the fruit of the Spirit is love, joy, peace, patience, forbearance, kindness, goodness, faithfulness, gentleness, and self-control (Galatians 5:19–23).

When we plug into the Holy Spirit, we truly become a sweet aroma to others, a breath of fresh Spirit-filled air to those who need to know the tenacious love of Jesus Christ (2 Corinthians 2:14–15).

Let's face it, putting our emotions aside when we have been wronged takes supernatural power! We cannot do it in our flesh. I shudder to think of all the times I have reacted in the flesh only to have to drop to my face before the Lord and ask Him to redeem my poor choices. However, I so appreciate that we serve a tenacious, loving, gracious, merciful God, who knows our weaknesses and is quick to forgive us when we confess. There are days when I think I have exhausted God's grace, only to be reminded through His Word that His mercies are new every morning and His grace is always sufficient. Oh, what a beautiful God we serve. I do also appreciate the conviction of the Holy Spirit when I have wronged someone. He quickens my heart to do my part in the healing process…which usually involves me eating crow and saying I am sorry. But after all, it's not about me…

What I have found is that *if I choose* ("if" being a conditional clause here) to surrender myself daily into the incredible loving arms of my heavenly Father and ask Him to create in me a clean heart and renew a right spirit within me, then I am good to go. When we submit and commit our day to God, then we realize early in the day that God has divine appointments for us throughout the day that *He* has orchestrated. These divine appointments give us the opportunity to shower tenacious love on those we might never encounter if it were up to us. Need to go to the doctor? Perhaps God is sending you to encourage the reception staff, nurses, maintenance and cleaning crew, and yes, even the doctor. Or perhaps you are stuck in line at the grocery store…what about praying for and encouraging those around you who may feel alone and need to be seen? Let's never forget that God works on epic levels and nothing is ever wasted in His economy… including your time. Let's look at those "inconveniences" as divine appointments and as opportunities to love others tenaciously.

Journal:

_____
_____
_____
_____
_____
_____
_____
_____
_____
_____
_____
_____
_____
_____
_____

CHAPTER THREE

Imitators

"Therefore be imitators of God as dear children. And walk in love, as Christ also has loved us and given Himself for us, an offering and a sacrifice to God for a sweet-smelling aroma" (Ephesians 5:1–2 NKJV).

As followers of Jesus Christ, we are called to be His imitators. What does this mean? It means that we are His representatives. With this revelation comes great responsibility.

Merriam-Webster's dictionary defines imitate as "to follow as a pattern, to be or appear like: resemble."

We were created to imitate our Creator, because we were made in His image. "Let us make mankind in our image, in our likeness, so that they may rule over the fish in the sea and the birds in the sky, over the livestock and all the wild animals, and over all the creatures that move along the ground" (Genesis 1:26 NIV).

Have you ever met someone who was such a tenacious lover it almost seemed unnatural? You know, those people who always find the bright spot and hone in on it, even in the midst of tragedy? I admire those individuals, and when I get to know them better, I realize that they are Jesus-loving people, and they are true imitators of His love. What makes them different? What makes them beautiful reflections of their Savior, Jesus Christ? *Choice.*

I want to tell you about one of the greatest examples of tenacious love that I have ever witnessed. It is a powerful example that has truly shaped my existence.

Several years ago my dear friend Sherry and her beloved husband, Dave, decided to go for a bike ride, as they often did together. For the first time ever, Sherry departed the house a few minutes before her husband. She had gotten to a place on the bike trail where she stopped to wait for him to join her so they could ride next to each other, just as they did every day. When she looked back, she saw Dave approaching and then was shocked to see him suddenly enveloped by a large cloud of dust. When he failed to come out of the cloud, she immediately rode back to see what was wrong. When she reached Dave, she saw to her horror that he had been struck by a vehicle driven by a woman who was driving irresponsi-bly, tragically taking Dave's life. All of this happened right in front of my precious friend.

As the days, months, and years unfolded, I watched my heartbroken friend choose to be a vessel of the Holy Spirit. In the world's eyes, she had every reason to respond in anger, resentment, and I dare to even say hatred, and to allow this tragedy to become a barrier between her and God...but that is not how Sherry responded. She *chose* to be a light in the darkness; in her very own darkest of nights, she *chose* to shine. She *chose* to cling to her Savior and allow Him to use her to imitate His love for the broken offender. Wow, that is tenacious love! Watching my friend go through the most dif-ficult of journeys was heartbreaking and yet overwhelmingly powerful. I watched her offer forgiveness in the courtroom to the very woman who took the most precious person away from her. I watched as she spoke words of life into this broken woman's life by granting her the greatest gift, forgiveness. She even bought the offender a Bible so she could get to know Jesus and His love for her. My dear friend chose to use her greatest pain as a platform to be a visual representation of Jesus Christ. My life, as well as countless other lives, was impacted on deep levels that day and was never the same.

Let's face it, we live in a world where being a Christian has been watered down. What does it truly mean to be Christian anymore? In antiquity, being a Christian meant that you were all in, sold out for Jesus, not compromising. Even to the death Christians remained faithful and their witness was not compromised. They left this earth giving honor to God.

Things have changed over time with how some of us Christians act. In fact, we—yes, I include myself in this— have from time to time been a stumbling block to those who desire to find Jesus Christ. In my earlier days as a believer, I didn't understand the brevity of what it meant to be a Christian. I just thought, *Hey, I am in the club, I gave my life to Jesus!* However, that step, as important as it was, was only the beginning. God wanted to transform me into His image, so when people saw me they could see the Father. Just as my dear friend showed the love of Jesus in her darkest hours.

Jesus' mission was always to bring glory to His heavenly Father. Jesus came to show the way to the Father (John 14:6) so everything He did reflected His Father's heart. Jesus was faithful to obey because He knew He was the image of His Father and anything He did would be a reflection of God. He knew it wasn't about Him, but about helping others reach His Father.

Wow, what if we all lived like that? With that divine perspective in everything we did... That would mean that every thought, word, or deed would be filtered through the "how would Jesus respond?" filter. That filter comes in the person of the Holy Spirit. He is faithful to instruct each of us, *if* we choose Him and allow Him full access into every area of our lives. This is the only way we can be authentic imitators of God.

Well, good news: if you have received Jesus Christ as your personal Savior, then the Lord is on board, my friend. And living a tenacious love life is very possible. However, surrendering to God every morning and asking Him to help you die to self is imperative. When you realize the importance of what it means to be Christian, that this life is not about you, then there is no room for the flesh. In fact, your flesh is against you and will take you down a path so far from tenacious love that the only thing at the end of the day that will be running through your head is how to do damage control. *Why did I do that?* and *How do I fix it?* Been there, done that, way too many times!

However, when you allow the Holy Spirit to have all of you by intentionally inviting Him in and relinquishing control every morning, then at the end of the day, when your head hits the pillow, you will know that He accomplished His will through you because you *chose* to surrender to the Holy Spirit, resulting in loving Him and loving others. And *that*, dear one, is what this life is all about.

Journal:

_____

_____

_____

_____

CHAPTER FOUR

The Love Scale

When you think about love, what comes to your mind? Is it a fluffy feeling? Romance? Friendship? We live in a day where we misuse the word love. I have been guilty of this myself. We say, "Oh, I love that dress," or "I just love that show!" But do we really know what true love is? God's love? The love that God has for us that we are called to demonstrate to each other? If we are going to embark on this tenacious love journey, then it is imperative and foundational that we understand what love is. There are several different types of love talked about in the Bible: *eros*, romantic love; *storge*, family love; *philia*, brotherly love; and *agape*, God's immeasurable love for humankind.

Until we receive the Holy Spirit, we cannot love with agape love, because it only comes with the power of God Himself. This is the kind of tenacious love that is unnatural, sacrificial. This is the love that we have access to *if* we choose to die to self and ask the Holy Spirit to love through us. This kind of love cannot be manifested in the flesh, it is *divine* and changes everything!

Jesus asked Peter, prior to Peter receiving the Holy Spirit, if he loved Him (*agape*), but Peter responded three times that he did love Him (*phileo*). Peter was incapable of any other love without the power of the Holy Spirit. Because God *is* love (1 John 4:8), apart from Him we cannot demonstrate it. We *must* plug into the power source…the Holy Spirit.

Just as God loves each one of His children uniquely and individually, we are called to do the same. You cannot put love in a box and tie it up with a pretty bow. Love can be hard, messy, and painful. It can mean confronting someone who has hurt you, or it can mean forgiving someone who has caused you the greatest amount of pain. It can mean getting in the muck and mire and helping a brother or sister who is lost and broken, and loving them even if they don't love you in return. It can mean loving people who, through petty things, shoot darts of dissension. And the list goes on… It's investing in the eternal, not expecting anything in return. It is *hard*…yet it is the most rewarding thing we can ever do, because it blesses God's heart and it shows the world *Him*!

When God first gave me this message, I was excited. "Wow, what a cool message!" I prayed. "Thanks, God!" Then He gave me opportunities to put the message into action. This is where it got D-I-F-F-I-C-U-L-T! I found that I was assaulted at every turn. It was exhausting! But God, in His infinite wisdom, grace, mercy, and sense of humor, took me to my journal and helped me work through the emotions, whether big, small, or even petty. He gave me a greatly needed perspective check. He called me to write down my emotions, and then He gently took me to Scripture where He showed me how to properly handle what I was facing. Jesus is *the* example, the Holy Spirit is *the* power. Now I had to make the choice of what I was going to do with that knowledge.

"See, I set before you today life and prosperity, death and destruction. For I command you today to love the LORD your God, to walk in obedience to him, and to keep his commands, decrees and laws; then you will live and increase, and the LORD your God will bless you in the land you are entering to possess" (Deuteronomy 30:15–16 NIV).

What Scripture Says about Selfless Love:

"But to you who are listening I say: *Love* your enemies, *do good* to those who hate you, *bless* those who curse you, *pray for* those who mistreat you. If someone slaps you on one cheek, turn to them the other also. If someone takes your coat, do not withhold your shirt from them. Give to everyone who asks you, and if anyone takes what belongs to you, do not demand it back. *Do to others as you would have them do to you.*

"If you love those who love you, what credit is that to you? Even sinners love those who love them. And if you do good to those who are good to you, what credit is that to you? Even sinners do that. And if you lend to those from whom you expect repayment, what credit is that to you? Even sinners lend to sinners, expecting to be repaid in full. But *love* your enemies, *do good* to them, and *lend* to them without expecting to get anything back. Then your reward will be great, and you will be children of the Most-High, because He is kind to the ungrateful and wicked. *Be merciful*, just as your Father is merciful" (Luke 6:27–36 NIV, emphasis added).

Prayer:

Lord, I love You. It is my desire to honor and glorify You through my life. As You know, my emotions can get the best of me somedays; however, I also realize that through the power of the Holy Spirit, You can change the trajectory and use the same emotions to show Yourself through me. Lord, I surrender these emotions and all the baggage that comes with them into Your loving hands. Please give me a divine perspective check and help me to love others just like You love me...*tenaciously.*

Reflection:

- *After learning about how much Jesus loves you and what measures He went through to demonstrate that love, how does that make you feel?*

- *What do you believe He is calling you to do with those feelings?*

Journal:

_____

_____

_____

_____

_____

_____

_____

_____

_____

_____

_____

_____

_____

_____

CHAPTER FIVE

Junk

I don't know about you, but I have some "junk" that I have been carrying around with me my entire life. This junk comes from being a broken and sinful individual living in a broken and sinful world. I don't like to ever think of myself as a victim, more as the recipient of others' poor choices, and many times my own. This happens any time we interact with people. Let's face it, people can hurt us, and we can hurt others; it's just the ramifications of sin. The truth is that broken and hurting people hurt other people. Meaning we all, yes *all*, have either been on the offenders' side, where we have hurt others, or on the receiving side where we have been the target. Why do we continue in this vicious cycle? The answer is simple: we are humans who have a sinful, fleshly nature. While our humanity may explain the why, it does not excuse us to live this way. Through Jesus' sacrifice on the cross and through His redemptive blood that was shed for all mankind, we now have a choice of what we are going to do with our junk. This study has been inspired by the Holy Spirit to help us choose to love, through His power and Jesus' example, in the most unreasonable and unfathomable way when we do not feel like it…tenaciously

Growing up, I was the third child out of four, and let's just say the most emotional one. I saw myself as the black sheep, if you will, and the rebel, the one that tested everything. I refused to be put into a mold, because I saw things differently. People and sports were my passion, and to be honest with you I really did not see the need for academia until adulthood. This was a problem. You see, I was the daughter of two very educated, intelligent, and highly motivated parents who thought I should be the same. Both had achieved great success in their lives and here they were stuck with this "wild child," as my mom put it. Navigating through my childhood was very difficult for me, because I only saw *my* needs and *my* hurt. I didn't know my worth in Christ or any identity outside of being different. Being raised in a house full of what I like to call "high achievers," I felt that I needed to perform in order to be loved. Because I was created with different passions and talents, I thought that I wasn't good enough. No matter how hard I tried, I just couldn't obtain what they wanted. I was lost and began questioning why I was even on this planet. Because I didn't fit in, something must be wrong with me.

However, as I grew up both physically and in my relationship with Jesus Christ, God took the scales off my eyes to reveal to me that I was actually different for a reason. He built me that way for a specific calling. I began to see my parents from His perspective and started to understand that my father and mother had struggles and "junk" of their own that they were trying to sort through. I stopped seeing them as those who were trying to squeeze me into a mold, rather as those who had hurts and pains themselves from their childhoods, and who were doing the best they could to make life better for their children. This is when I realized it wasn't about me, it was about giving my mom and dad grace as they were working through their own brokenness to try to provide a different life for their children.

This is the cycle, and sometimes we get stuck. We just go around and around in the same generational brokenness, chalking it up to our upbringing. This, my friend, is a choice. You have the power through the Holy Spirit to be freed. All you need to do is ask God to help break the chains and then intentionally choose to walk in a new way He has shown you through His Word. Change is possible; you can do it!

As we ask God to help us work through our own junk, we need to allow others to work through their own, without judgment. While we are seeking God, we can ask Him to help us understand why others act the way they do.

I like to say "KYP": know your people.

This doesn't mean we stay in abusive relationships and allow ourselves to be targets, verbally or physically, but it does mean that we can help others by taking them to the throne room of Christ in prayer. You see, it wasn't until I started praying for my parents that my heart was softened towards them and the scales came off my eyes. I stopped trying to judge them and started praying for their brokenness and pain. Everybody has pain, friends, everyone is coming from something. Yes, even our parents and authority figures are human and have brokenness. So, what will we *choose* to do with that? Will we choose to hang on to bitterness and blame? Or will we choose to forgive them and run to Jesus and hand them over to Him in prayer? After all, He is the only One who can heal the offender's brokenness as well as ours.

I am sure you have heard the saying "One man's junk is another man's treasure." What if we choose to ask God to turn our junk into treasure? What if good could actually come out of our darkest times instead of manifesting as insecurities? The truth is, God does turn our junk into treasure! "And we know that in *all things God works for the good* of those who love him, who have been called according to his purpose" (Romans 8:28 NIV, emphasis added). And what if everything that we have gone through actually had a purpose? Well, my dear friend, it does! Second Corinthians 1:3–4 (NIV) says, "Praise be to the God and Father of our Lord Jesus Christ, the Father of compassion and the God of all comfort, who comforts us in all our troubles, so that we can comfort those in any trouble with the comfort we ourselves receive from God."

If we allow the Holy Spirit to work in us, then our most painful days will actually be used to help others through theirs. That is God's economy: your greatest struggles become your greatest ministries. Your pain has a purpose in the hands of our mighty God. Isn't that great news?!

It is time to let go of those emotions that have held us captive for way too long. Remember, broken and hurt people hurt people, but redeemed people help free people through the power of the Holy Spirit. Keep praying and watch Him work; He is doing *big* things.

STOP

Reflection:

- *What relationships do you feel were the most difficult for you growing up?*

- *Are those people still affecting you to this day? If so, in what ways?*

- *Ask the Holy Spirit what He wants to teach you through your junk.*

- *How is God able to turn your junk into treasure to help others?*

Write your prayer to God asking Him, by the power of the Holy Spirit, to lead, empower, and anoint you as you surrender all the pain and insecurities from your past. Remember, in the hands of our tenacious, loving heavenly Father, our junk becomes His treasure.

Ask God to give you a Scripture verse that you can hang onto to encourage you in this area.

What person or people is God calling you to pray for?

Journal: What will you choose?

Journal:

_____
_____
_____
_____
_____
_____
_____
_____
_____

CHAPTER SIX

Insecurities

"Oh, for the love! Why did I respond that way? Why did I let *that* get to me?"

Do these words sound familiar? Have they ever run through your mind and possibly out of your mouth? I have to be honest and tell you that these words and thoughts have run through my head most of my life, until I finally took them to God and asked Him to show me why certain things set me off and why I am sometimes the target of others' negative responses.

It's not an easy process when God calls us to search our hearts, only to reveal a secret closet we have kept locked for years. You know those places you don't want to talk about, those hidden pains that result in bondage and insecurities? Let's face it, it is much easier to stay in denial and pretend that we have it all together. Or is it? What ends up happening? Something eventually sets us off and opens that closet of insecurities, revealing a monster of emotions. How do we stop this vicious cycle from continuing? The answer seems simple, but the process is far from it. It takes an intentional decision to sit with God and give Him the key to the "closet."

I have been deeply impacted by the powerful little book by Robert Boyd Munger, *My Heart—Christ's Home*. In his book, Munger highlights the importance of letting God have full access to one's heart. After all, if we are wanting to be imitators of Jesus and live a life reflecting His tenacious love, it is imperative to give God the key to our entire "home." Yes, even that closet that you think nobody else knows about.

I remember clearly the day when I was finally ready to give Jesus full access to my closet. If I am being honest, I must tell you it was *years* after receiving Him as my Savior. That day He stirred my heart to take this life-changing step. "My child, if you want Me to help with your pain and insecurities, then may I have the key to your closet?"

I have to admit, I was terrified…terrified of disappointing Him with what I kept in the closet: anger, jealousy, poor decisions, shame, and a range of other emotions that I didn't want to deal with. Then tenacious love happened. He gently led me to Scripture that reassured me of His unconditional love and reminded me why He chose to do what He did: "But God demonstrates His own love toward us, in that while we were still sinners, Christ died for us" (Romans 5:8 NKJV).

The reality was He knew what was in my closet; it was not going to be a shock to Him. He had already forgiven me the second I confessed these things to Him years ago (1 John 1:9). He revealed to me that the insecurities and pains hidden in my closet were once open wounds that had become part of me. However, in His hands they would move from open wounds to scars. Open wounds still hurt and can paralyze us in the way of insecurities, but scars tell a story of healing. Our pains and insecurities can become beautiful glory stories in the hands of our Creator, bringing beauty from ashes. Wow, what a beautiful revelation!

His next stirring question forced me to deal with my real issue. He asked "Do you trust Me?" Ouch…as one who likes control and has severe trust issues, He knew this was where the rubber met the road. You see, up until that time I believed *in* God and had given my life to Jesus, but I had not fully known His character or trusted Him enough to hand over my deepest pains. This was a huge relational crossroad in my life. Would I continue to pretend everything was fine and cover my closet of pain and insecurities with a pretty painting, or would I surrender my greatest fears, pains, and insecurities to the One who gave up everything for me, the only One who truly had the power to transform my closet of pain and shame into a beautiful room full of light and purpose?

"For it is by grace you have been saved, through faith—and this is not from yourselves, it is the gift of God—not by works, so that no one can boast" (Ephesians 2:8 NIV).

I finally understood that His grace was an unmerited divine gift, and if I truly trusted Him, then it was time. So, I decided to surrender the key. I felt as if I led Him to my closet, took down the facade that I thought was hiding the door, and invited Him to enter. Sheer joy enveloped me as He reminded me that I didn't need to be ashamed because there is now no condemnation for those in Christ Jesus (Romans 8:1). As the Holy Spirit ministered to me through this truth, He also revealed it was now time to trust Him with the healing process. You see, I had been schlepping around chains of insecurities for most of my life and was exhausted. I didn't want to feel the emotions that came with them any longer. I needed help. So I asked Him to remove all the lies, chains, and any residue that the enemy could use to ensnare me through insecurities. I gave Him full permission to scrub every nook and cranny of my closet with bleach and a toothbrush. And guess what? He jumped in and started the process immediately...but He also explained to me that this was going to be a lifelong process that required an ongoing intentional choice on my part to run to Him every time I felt insecure. I now needed to stop...pray...filter.

My eyes were opened that day. It's as if the Holy Spirit Himself removed blinders that had up until that point only directed my eyes to my faults, leaving me with incredible insecurities. But now my gaze was directed to the Author and Finisher of my faith, Jesus Christ (Hebrews 12:2), and with that refocus came another divine perspective change. Each time I experienced emotions from insecurities, I would run to Him and ask Him to replace them with truth found in His Word. And He did. When I felt regret, He led me to His Word. When I felt shame, He led me to His Word. When I felt jealousy or anger or any other emotion that came from these insecurities, He led me to His Word. Through these encounters with Him I learned no matter how bad things may appear there was always a way to handle them that would bring Him glory and keep me from going back to being ensnared with emotional chains. But what I learned was His way is narrow, difficult, and countercultural.

Through my experience and divine perspective change the Holy Spirit has called me to show the same grace and mercy towards others as He shows me. Let's face it, everyone has an insecurity closet and will react from time to time because of it. Pain and insecurities from living in this world may come in many different forms and leave open wounds. Even though we may feel we have worked through them, whether it was on our end where we needed to ask God for forgiveness or perhaps as the recipient of another person's pain, the enemy can use these encounters to deceive us into believing that we are not loved, forgiven, useful, valued, or worthy. However, when we run to our beautiful Savior every time they surface, He is faithful to put His salve of truth on our scars and remind us of our identity and value in Him... which is priceless.

Our tenacious, loving God is patiently waiting to be invited in to do a deep cleaning in your life. When you decide to hand over the key to your closet, you will experience a beautiful transformational and repurposing work.

Are you ready to hand Him the key to your closet?

Reflection:

- *What's in your "closet"?*

- *What insecurities do you struggle with?*

- *What is God calling you to do with them?*

Write your prayer to God asking Him, by the power of the Holy Spirit, to give you wisdom, peace, and joy as you surrender your insecurities to Him.

Remember, your identity is now in Him and you can live in that confidence daily! You've got this because He's got you.

Journal: What will you choose?

Journal:

_____
_____
_____
_____
_____
_____
_____
_____
_____
_____
_____
_____
_____
_____
_____
_____
_____
_____
_____
_____
_____
_____
_____
_____
_____
_____
_____
_____
_____
_____

_____
_____
_____
_____
_____
_____
_____
_____
_____
_____
_____
_____
_____
_____
_____
_____
_____
_____
_____
_____
_____
_____
_____
_____
_____
_____
_____

Munger, R. B. (1951). My Heart—Christ's Home. IVP.

CHAPTER SEVEN

Who Told You That?
Where Is It Written?

Ever desire to run away from yourself? I mean *really* try to escape yourself? You know those days when your mind seems to be your worst enemy. "I can't do that!" "I am not good enough for this." "I need to look like that or think like this or achieve this or avoid that..." Oh my stars, HELP! STOP THE TRAIN! This is a place I find myself in from time to time, and if I am being completely honest, some days are worse than others. However, I love that the Holy Spirit is our Teacher, our Counselor, our Instructor of truth, and our very present help in time of need. He is faithful to help redirect us if we choose to allow Him full access.

The other day I was beating myself up in my thought life, I mean it was a *brawl*. My flesh was trying to stir up emotions by bombarding me with lie after lie, while my spirit was trying to grasp on to every truth that I could. I struggled, I wrestled, I felt like I was losing the battle until God whispered these incredible words to me: "Who told you that? Where is it written?" Wow, time out! Yes, where did I get that thought? And where *is* it written in God's Word? Is it Him telling me that I need to be something I am not? No. Where does God tell me that I need to do more and work harder to be something? Where in His Word does it say that I am junk? Well? Where? Nowhere. These thoughts are *not* from Him, yet my emotions seem to be powered by them. Wow, Houston, we have a BIG problem!"

You can imagine the freedom I felt when my precious Lord whispered those life-changing words in my spirit. These thoughts were not reality, but rather the enemy's ploy to defeat me, to use myself to take me out of the game. Remember that the enemy cannot steal us from God, but he can try to hit us so hard that sometimes we begin believing the lies about ourselves. However, these words of freedom from our Creator give us an arsenal that we can truly use to cut the enemy off at the knees, *if* we choose to use it. The truth is that the enemy, or "tempter," used this very tactic in the Garden when he planted the seed of doubt and discontentment in Eve's mind. Eve listened, pondered, and then acted on the lie. She knew God but chose to believe a lie from something she didn't even know. Oh, how often we do the same.

"Now the serpent was more crafty than any of the wild animals the LORD God had made. He said to the woman, 'Did God really say, "You must not eat from any tree in the garden"?' The woman said to the serpent, 'We may eat fruit from the trees in the garden, but God did say, "You must not eat fruit from the tree that is in the middle of the garden, and you must not touch it, or you will die."'

"'You will not certainly die,' the serpent said to the woman. 'For God knows that when you eat from it your eyes will be opened, and you will be like God, knowing good and evil.'

"When the woman saw that the fruit of the tree was good for food and pleasing to the eye, and also desirable for gaining wisdom, she took some and ate it. She also gave some to her husband, who was with her, and he ate it. Then the eyes of both of them were opened, and they realized they were naked; so they sewed fig leaves together and made coverings for themselves.

"Then the man and his wife heard the sound of the LORD God as he was walking in the garden in the cool of the day, and they hid from the LORD God among the trees of the garden. But the LORD God called to the man, 'Where are you?' He answered, 'I heard you in the garden, and I was afraid because I was naked; so I hid.' And he said, 'Who told you that you were naked? Have you eaten from the tree that I commanded you not to eat from?' The man said, 'The woman you put here with me—she gave me some fruit from the tree, and I ate it.' Then the LORD God said to the woman, 'What is this you have done?' The woman said, 'The serpent deceived me, and I ate'" (Genesis 3:1–11 NIV).

Just as Eve and Adam were deceived by the serpent in the garden, we are deceived today. Every time we "bite" on the lie that the enemy tries to lure us with, we get caught and ensnared by the emotions that ensue. Think about it, how often do we push aside God, the One who built each of us individually, in order to fit in or please someone else? Where is it written that we have to wear this or weigh that? Where is it written that I have to have this education or achieve some earthly accolades to feel accepted or loved? Where is it written that we can't have laugh lines or imperfections? Or where is it written that I have to go one thousand miles per hour every day to try to please everyone? Where is it written? Who told us that? I am going to be real honest here, I don't know about you, but I am tired of buying the lie. I am exhausted from trying to measure up to...what? Who? I don't even know who "that" is anymore. All I know is that my thought life can take the bait of lies and run full steam ahead with it. It is my opinion and experience that riding that train will end up taking me to a destination of despair, brokenness, loss of identity, and exhaustion. However, good news: we can stop this deception train for good by being intentional about where we get our information. God's Word tells us the truth…and that, my friends, is the freedom train we should buy a ticket for.

Let's face it, if we are going to live this tenacious love journey, we need to know what the tenacious One is telling us. This can only happen when we take those rogue thoughts, which lead us down a path of deception, captive to Him and find out what He has to say (2 Corinthians 10:5). This can only be done when we seek Him through His Word, the Bible. We tend to listen to others' opinions rather than the opinion of the One who created us. This has been a huge stumbling block in my life and I wonder how many victories I would have won in the Lord if I had asked Him to show me His perspective when it came to myself. After all, He is the Designer, and He knows each of us better than we know ourselves.

My grandson Cooper, who is three, really enjoys going to church and loves Jesus. Every Sunday I ask him what he learned at church that day, and his response has always been the same. "I learned about Jesus." However, last Sunday when I asked him the question, his response was different. He said, "Don't eat apples!" You see, he was learning about the tempter and the choice Adam and Eve made in the garden. His response to the lesson was to "stay away from apples, they are bad." While my precious little man had not quite grasped the entire depth of the message, there was still power in his perspective. The enemy used a piece of fruit to lure and deceive Adam and Eve and is still using the same tactic today.

The enemy knows what bait to use on each one of us that stirs the insecurities in our lives. The truth is that the "apple" can come in many shapes and forms: power, materialism, lust, self-focus, food, drink, attention, and so many others. This is why it is imperative to know our vulnerabilities and areas of weakness and then to commit them to God. We can ask Him to be our help and refuge in these times of need. In actuality, He is the *only* way we can defeat the enemy and not take the bait. It all begins when we see that bright, shiny lure floating past us and realize the fisherman is the deceiver.

"For God has not given us a spirit of fear, but of power and of love and of a sound mind" (2 Timothy 1:7 NKJV).

Reflection:

- *Just as Eve took the "bait" of deception in the garden, in what area is the enemy fishing for you? Are you "biting"?*

- *Do you feel that you are in bondage in your thought life?*

- *Ask the Holy Spirit to reveal the truth about yourself.*

- *What truth is the Holy Spirit giving you?*

- *What is He calling you to do?*

Journal: What will you choose?

Journal:

_____
_____
_____
_____
_____
_____
_____
_____
_____
_____
_____
_____
_____
_____
_____
_____
_____
_____
_____
_____
_____
_____
_____
_____

TENACIOUS LOVE

CHAPTER EIGHT

Are You My Friend or Not? I Am Confused.

What do you do when you know that people are going to betray you? You know those people who, the second you walk away, will talk behind your back. What do you do with those people? Well, honestly, in my flesh, I can react in an emotional state that will most likely result in me doing the same thing to the offender. We as humans tend to justify this by "venting" to another person. Interestingly, the very thing we are upset about is the very thing we end up doing in return. Why am I thinking about a plank in my eye right now?!

Years ago, I coached competitive soccer. I was the kind of coach that asked the players what their goals were and then proceeded to give them a plan of action to help them reach their lofty heights. This was a draw to many players who wanted a coach to help them prepare for a higher level of play. While overall my coaching experience was amazing, there was this one individual that I chose to allow to change it all. I was warned by other coaches about her mother. She had a reputation for dissolving teams by stabbing the coach in the back. However, I disregarded their warnings because I like to establish my own opinions based on my own relation-ships, and I offered this player a position on my team. After all, she was very talented and hardworking and I felt should not be punished for the mother's indiscretions.

While I did my best to love this woman and make her feel like she was part of the team, she ended up choosing to continue to do what she had done in the past. She found something that she didn't agree with and behind my back stirred up dissension, resulting in factions on the team. I was upset. All she had to do was talk to me and I would have explained my choice and reassured her that she was a valued part of the team. So what did I do? I acted on my emotions and let her offense penetrate my heart. The painful thing was that this woman's choice to act the way she did ended up separating the team, resulting in me choosing to leave the coaching profession for many years. Over time, God revealed to me that this woman was operating out of great pain. She had lost a child at a young age and was angry, and everyone who got in her way felt it.

I believe we all have stories like this where we acted out or where we were the recipient of someone else's actions. While we may be stuck and holding on to the pain associated with such encounters, we do not have to let them dictate how we respond in the future. You see, I ran away from a profession that I loved because I didn't want to "deal" with any more people like the one who hurt me. Let's just say the enemy won that one in my life.

However, I absolutely love it when we look at Jesus' example and are given a different, holy choice when facing these tricky relationships.

"When Jesus had said these things, He was troubled in spirit, and testified and said, 'Most assuredly, I say to you, one of you will betray Me'" (John 13:21 NKJV).

I don't know about you, but sometimes I forget that while Jesus was 100 percent God, He was also 100 percent human. When we read John 13, I can't help but consider how Jesus must have felt. While He and the disciples were in the upper room celebrating the Passover feast prior to His arrest, Jesus *knew* that He was going to be betrayed by Judas, one whom He considered a friend. Wow, do you think Jesus knows exactly how we feel? Absolutely! But what Jesus *chose* to do in order to love Judas tenaciously, even with this knowledge, is truly inspirational and powerful!

"Jesus answered, 'Those who have had a bath need only to wash their feet; their whole body is clean. And you are clean, though not every one of you.' For he knew who was going to betray him, and that was why he said not everyone was clean. When he had finished washing their feet, he put on his clothes and returned to his place. 'Do you understand what I have done for you?' he asked them. 'You call me "Teacher" and "Lord," and rightly so, for that is what I am. Now that I, your Lord and Teacher, have washed your feet, you also should wash one another's feet. I have set you an example that you should do as I have done for you. Very truly I tell you, no servant is greater than his master, nor is a messenger greater than the one who sent him. Now that you know these things, you will be blessed if you do them'" (John 13:10–17 NIV).

Even though He knew that Judas was going to be His betrayer, Jesus chose to treat Judas the same as the others. He could have ratted out Judas or refused to wash his feet, yet He didn't. Why? Because Jesus was the embodiment of love and He was giving us the most powerful example of what tenacious love looks like. Some may say, "Well, Jesus could love like that because He was God, He had the power to do it." But friend, don't you and I have the same power through the Holy Spirit? Remember, Jesus left each one of us with this tremendous gift so we would have the supernatural power to follow His example.

I often think back to my encounter with the one who hurt me on the soccer team. What would have happened if I had chosen to see her and acknowledge her pain from the get-go? What would have happened if I had chosen to put my own emotion aside like Jesus did and love her tenaciously through His power? While I will never have that opportunity again, I have purpose in my heart to continue to pray for this individual and ask God to bathe her in His healing love, wherever she may be. I also ask Him, with the direction and empowerment of the Holy Spirit, to help me choose to love the offender as He continues to love me.

Reflection:

- *Just like Jesus chose to love Judas, who is God calling you to love in your life?*
- *How is the Holy Spirit calling you to love this person?*
- *Have you been a Judas to someone?*
- *Ask the Holy Spirit to teach you how to respond to this knowledge.*

Journal: What will you choose?

Journal:

_____

_____

_____

_____

_____

_____

_____

_____

_____

_____

_____

_____

_____

_____

_____

_____

_____

_____

_____

_____

_____

_____

_____

_____

_____

_____

_____

_____

_____

ARE YOU MY FRIEND OR NOT? I AM CONFUSED.

CHAPTER NINE

When It Rains, It Pours

Ever have those days, weeks, months, or sometimes years when it feels like everywhere you turn you are getting rained on? These seasons of life can be downright depressing. Oh, how we long to be in the sunshine and escape the rain! While the sunshine may be good for us emotionally and physically, making us happy by giving our body vitamin D, I have come to learn, over time, that rain can be just as beneficial, yet it is not always as pleasant.

Oh the rain... Let's face it, friends, there are times in our lives when, through no fault of our own, we find ourselves in a downpour of hardship and discouragement. I will never forget the day God taught me the value of the rain. I have a very special place at my house where I go every morning to meet with my precious Savior. It's a small courtyard that is surrounded by life: roses, grapevines, ivy, and a beautiful water feature. It is a place where even the critters come to take nourishment before starting their day. It truly is my inner sanctum, my haven. One morning when I was out reading my Bible, I noticed it starting to drizzle. It was a soft rain almost like mist from the sea. I found myself getting giddy! I am the kind of "kid" that likes to dance in the rain and jump into every puddle I find. I just love water!

While I was enraptured by these feelings of bliss, the Lord softly whispered in my spirit, "Are you thankful for the rain?"

"Oh *yes*, Lord, I am so thankful for this rain!"

"No, my child, are you thankful for the *rain*?"

It was then that He gently revealed that we will have rainy days in the form of hardships: physical, emotional, financial, relational, or perhaps even in our identity. The rain will come. Then He led me to this passage in Scripture:

"'My grace is sufficient for you, for my power is made perfect in weakness.' Therefore I will boast all the more gladly about my weaknesses, so that Christ's power may rest on me. That is why, for Christ's sake, I delight in weaknesses, in insults, in hardships, in persecutions, in difficulties. For when I am weak, then I am strong" (2 Corinthians 12:9–10 NIV).

While I have to admit, this took the giddiness right out of my sail, it was incredibly timely and hopeful. Little did I know this beautiful message from my Lord was preparing me for one of the most difficult seasons of my life. One month later I would experience a small stroke that would take me down an emotional path of fear, pain, financial strain, loss of identity, and a gamut of other emotions. *But* God, in His faithfulness, used these "rainy" days to give me the most amazing nuggets of tenacious love and purpose. I recall a powerful, life-changing conversation with my dear friend Michelle in which she said, "I am so jealous! God is going to teach you the most amazing things through this journey!"

Wow, was she right! You see, dear friends, I came to realize there are treasures that we can only discover while in the "trenches" of life. Those places where we feel so weak, helpless, out of control, and alone, where only the Lord Himself can reach us, pull us out, and help us stand again on solid ground. However, one thing is for sure, we never come out of the trenches the same; some may come out better, while others may come out bitter. What makes the difference? Jesus and purpose. I learned, through many months of suffering physically and emotionally, that if we choose to surrender these times to the Lord, He is faithful to give us what we need to not only get through the rain but to grow through the rain. We all know there is nothing like rain water to help our gardens grow; the same results happen to us spiritually when we welcome the rain and allow God full access during these uncertain and difficult times.

I would later come to discover that with surrender, God would give me a purpose through the rain. He showed me that our rainy days can be used to love tenaciously, even in our lowest times when we feel we have nothing left to give. I truly believe our greatest form of worship is when we worship while we are suffering, I also wholeheartedly believe it takes us to a depth of intimacy with Him that only happens in our darkest times…in the trenches.

I experienced this intimacy when I surrendered my emotions and pain to my sweet Savior and asked Him to do what He wanted to do through this storm. It was then that He showed me His purpose in it. You see, up until that point I thought it was all about me. "I am scared, I am worried, I am in pain…" Once I took the "I am" out of it and surrendered to the Great I AM, then my perspective changed and it all became clear. He taught me my suffering wasn't just about me. Sure, He was teaching me more about myself and His character, but there was so much more. He wanted to use it for something greater; however, He didn't minimize my suffering. He met me in the lowest place and held me until I was ready to move through the storm.

I am sure you have heard the saying "Sometimes God calms the storm but other times it's the child He calms in the midst of the storm." I have found this to be true; however, there is more…so much more! You see, while He calms the child in the storm, He also is repurposing the pain. Nothing is ever wasted in God's economy…especially pain! What I watched Him do through this time was straight-up divine. He showed me that because of my situation, everyone who loved me was going to Him in prayer. I recall a dear friend calling me and telling me a loved one of theirs, someone I didn't even know, who had never prayed before, was turning to God and praying for me! Wow, that was a game changer for me! It was then that God showed me the ripple effect. He was using my suffering to bring others to Him and doing powerful things that I may never know about…*all for His glory*. He once again brought to mind Romans 8:28 (NKJV): "And we know that all things work together for good to those who love God, to those who are the called according to His purpose."

It became evident at that point that I was on a mission. He opened up doors for me to be seen at one of the top hospitals in the nation, the Mayo Clinic, and encouraged me that I was to love and encourage others who were experiencing the same emotions. He reminded me He made me to do this and was strategically sending me to those who needed encouragement. He knew there were many at the medical facility without hope and who needed to be "seen" and loved. He saw their need and He chose me to go. *That* was the mission, and I was humbled at the opportunity.

It was then He gave me the idea to take chocolate and small cards with words of encouragement to my doctors, patients, nurses, maintenance workers, and shuttle drivers. Let's just say anyone whom the Holy Spirit led me to, He loved on. You see, it was *His* power through my weakness that helped me to see past myself. If it were just me, I would have been found in the fetal position in the corner crying out, "Oh, woe is me!" This, my friends, was Him, all Him! However, He allowed me the privilege of being the vessel in this divine partnership, all because I chose to surrender my "rain" to Him. Don't get me wrong, there were several times I cried myself to sleep and my emotions got the better of me. There were times I lost focus and fell into the fears of the unknowns, only to be gently reminded by the Holy Spirit that we serve a God who is always with us (Joshua 1:9) and who is faithful to finish what He began (Philippians 1:6).

At the end of my medical journey, it was discovered I had a hole in my heart that was unique and unlike any other. It was positional and only opened upon certain stressful physical positions. Because this hole in my heart opened up and threw something into my brain, God was able to love and encourage others through me. This experience changed the way I look at the rain. I have come to look for the "rainbows" and silver linings, because our tenacious, loving God is always there working behind the scenes on epic levels.

I have to say I find our God so whimsical. You see, I have always prayed for a holy heart, and my God literally gave me one. He showed me through a "holy heart" He and I can still dance in the rain.

Reflection:

- *Do you find yourself in a "rainy" season? Explain.*

- *How is the rain affecting your life? Have you been becoming bitter or better? Explain.*

- *What promises from God's Word are you choosing to hang on to during the storm?*

- *Stop and think about all those around you right now. Ask the Holy Spirit to show you your divine purpose through your suffering. What is He showing you?*

- *Do you know someone else who is going through a "rainy" season?*

- *Ask the Holy Spirit to teach you how to come alongside them and support them. Write the ideas He has given you.*

Suffering is difficult and we are not meant to go through it alone. Remember, you have a tenacious, loving Savior who is with you in the trenches. He sees you and desires you to run to Him with all your pain and let Him hold you. Don't be afraid to be raw and be real because He will never leave you or forsake you and will be faithful to take your pain and repurpose it...if you choose to surrender it to Him.

Journal: What will you choose?

Journal:

_____

_____

_____

_____

_____

_____

_____

_____

_____

_____

_____

_____

_____

_____

_____

_____

_____

_____

_____

_____

_____

_____

_____

_____

_____

_____

_____

_____

_____

_____

_____

CHAPTER TEN

Does Everything Have to Be a Competition?

Do you ever feel when you are in the presence of certain individuals that they see you as a competitor? You know those people who you just seem to set off by being around you? These are tricky people, and to be honest, ones I struggle with. You know why? Because I too can be one of those people. Especially when I take my eyes off of my Savior and put them on myself. Let's face it, the majority of us were raised to compete; whether we compete for attention, compete for validation, compete to get our own way, compete to be "right," or compete just because we want to be number one...we compete. We know every competition has a winner and a loser, and because of that knowledge, when we see others as competition, we end up seeing them as a threat. How can we love others tenaciously when we are so focused on competing? The answer is quite simple: we can't. Let's get real, it's extremely difficult to work on a relationship when the other person sees you as a threat or when we ourselves see others through the same lens. What do we do with *that*?

Think about how Jesus was treated by the Pharisees. These individuals were so "threatened" by Jesus' claims, message, power, influence, and love for all people that they wanted to kill Him. Their emotions were straight-up out of control! Not one of their emotions was fueled by righteousness, but rather by pride. So, how did Jesus respond?

"And He entered the synagogue again, and a man was there who had a withered hand. So they watched Him closely, whether He would heal him on the Sabbath, so that they might accuse Him. And He said to the man who had the withered hand, 'Step forward.' Then He said to them, 'Is it lawful on the Sabbath to do good or to do evil, to save life or to kill?' But they kept silent. And when He had looked around at them with anger, being grieved by the hardness of their hearts, He said to the man, 'Stretch out your hand.' And he stretched it out, and his hand was restored as whole as the other. Then the Pharisees went out and immediately plotted with the Herodian's against Him, how they might destroy Him" (Mark 3:1–6 NKJV).

Jesus was an incredible example of persisting in His existence. Knowing the Pharisees saw Him as a threat and realizing their hearts were hard towards Him, He became angry and then He grieved for their state. However, He didn't stop there. He also saw the man with the withered hand. Jesus put the man's need to be healed before what the Pharisees thought was most important, their law. Jesus loved them enough to confront them, to share the truth with them, and to stand up to them. Is that tenacious love? I don't know about you, but I believe if we are caught up in something that can lead us astray from the truth, then confrontation *is* love. Even if it results in the other person becoming offended. Jesus demonstrated that love to every person in the synagogue; however, what they chose to do with that love was on them…it was their choice. Many of them chose, because they felt threatened, to falsely accuse Jesus. Their feelings and emotions were used as an instrument by the enemy to plot Jesus' death. The saddest part is that their hearts were so hard and fixed on Jesus being a threat that they missed the One standing in front of them who was actually *the* Messiah they had been waiting for. "He came to His own, and His own did not receive Him" (John 1:11 NKJV).

What a heartbreaking choice they made. Here they were in the presence of God Himself. They had just watched Him perform a miracle that resulted in a man being healed, yet they walked away with anger and resentment towards Jesus because His actions challenged their authority. Wow, isn't this what happens to us when we see others as threats? We miss out on the beautiful work that God is doing because we can only see them as threats, as competition. Just think about how Jesus must have felt. After all, what did He do wrong? Nothing. He was innocent. But the Pharisees could not see past their law and their offense to see the Messiah or the hurting man who was in the same room who desperately needed Jesus' touch.

Sometimes, my friend, we find ourselves being on the offended side and being hurt by others who can't see past their own self. The truth is that the person who has hurt you by treating you as a threat is a person that God loves just as much as He loves you and me. Whether they're coming from a place of insecurity or pride or something else, they believe this to be their reality. This can leave others around them feeling assaulted. But just like Jesus, we do not have to be paralyzed by our emotions. We can continue to persist in our existence. How do we move past this offense? First, we must remember that the enemy is the enemy, not the person. Then we must take the "offender" straight to Jesus in prayer and ask Him to give us His perspective towards the individual in order for us to understand their pain. The beautiful thing about running to Him is that He knows the heart of each person. And as we run to Him and ask the Holy Spirit to give us His discerning Spirit, then, and only then, can we begin to see the person's pain and struggles. At that point we become vessels that the Holy Spirit can use to tenaciously love the individual as only God can.

Now the tough question: what if *we* are the offenders and the Pharisees? I cannot tell you how many times I have fallen into the "competition" trap only to realize that I allowed myself to be ensnared by my insecurities. Whether the other person's accomplishments made me feel inadequate or jealous, either way, I *chose* to see them as competition instead of celebrating what God was doing in and through them. I chose to allow my fleshly emotions to overshadow the goodness that God was allowing in that person's life. Just like the Pharisees, I have made heartbreaking choices. But thank God that He loves us way too much to allow us to stay in those places.

Reflection:

Ask the Holy Spirit to help you see the other person as one who is unique and a treasure from God, not competition. Ask Him to give you the ability to celebrate with others and not allow the enemy to stir up fleshly emotions.

- *Do you see anyone as a threat?*

- *Does anyone see you as a threat?*

- *How is this affecting you?*

- *What is the Holy Spirit stirring you to do?*

Journal: What will you choose?

Journal:

_____

_____

_____

_____

_____

_____

_____

_____

_____

_____

_____

_____

_____

_____

_____

_____

_____

_____

_____

_____

_____

_____

DOES EVERYTHING HAVE TO BE A COMPETITION?

CHAPTER ELEVEN

I Am Sorry, That's Not on My Agenda Today

What do you see when you look around you? Do you see needs? And what do you do when you see so much need? Does the need evoke emotions of compassion, empathy, or judgment? Let's be honest, it can almost be overwhelming when we see how many people are in need of help.

I don't know about you, but I can become desensitized to the needs around me when I am not intentional about submitting myself to the Holy Spirit. Every night on the news there seems to be another tragedy and another heart-breaking story. There are times when I feel I have become so accustomed to seeing the beggar on the street that I can drive by without even stopping to think of the person behind the need. Let's face it, sometimes we become judges of the "least of these." I am going to be transparent. I believe, dear friends, that we (me being the worst offender here) sometimes forget who we truly are and the responsibility we have been given. The truth is we are *all* broken, we are *all* in need of love, and it is by the grace of God alone that we have been given what we have. "Every good and perfect gift is from above" (James 1:17 NIV). It is all from Him and belongs to Him.

I will never forget the day God called me to step out of my comfort zone and perceive, not just "see," a homeless individual in need. Up until that point I was afraid of what might happen to me if I got out of my car and engaged with "them." You can see the problem: a skewed perspective that was all about me. I was only "seeing" the need and allowing the what-ifs to keep me from loving tenaciously.

On this day, I was running errands with my kids and we decided to stop at Taco Bell for lunch. They were hungry and we were in a hurry; I thought I didn't really have time for anything else on my agenda that day. I was going to hit the drive-through and be on our way, but God had a different plan for us. As we drove into the parking lot we noticed a man sitting between two dumpsters. It was apparent that he was in great need…of what, I had no idea, until the Holy Spirit stirred me to buy him lunch. I was just going to run through the drive-through and order a couple extra tacos and hand them out the window, say the canned, "God bless you," and be on my way. But God stopped me in my tracks. Don't you love it when the Holy Spirit penetrates your heart and cuts through the self-focus with the powerful message of "It's not about you. I am giving you an opportunity through this divine detour but you need to work with me here!"

The next few moments seemed surreal as I pulled into a parking space, unloaded my middle school-aged children, and went inside to buy lunch. I sat my cherubs down to eat and felt the Lord moving me outside to the man we had seen between the dumpsters. What transpired next was straight-up divine! The Holy Spirit through me engaged with this precious individual, whose name was Jack, and revealed his brokenness. You see, he thought nobody saw him, he thought that his life was a mistake, he felt he had no purpose, he felt hopeless. Yet God in His beautiful compassion and tenacious love saw His hurting child and chose to use His other broken and unworthy child—me—to be His hands and feet.

Think about it, what if we chose to invite Jesus into every moment of our day and asked Him, through the power of the Holy Spirit, to give us His divine perspective as we went through our day? Do you think we would see others like Jack all around us and perceive what the Holy Spirit would like to do through us? I am confident in saying *yes*! That's what Jesus did. He saw those in need physically and spiritually. That is His heart. And guess what? He told us that we are actually serving and loving Him when we do this.

"When the Son of Man comes in his glory, and all the holy angels with him, then he will sit on the throne of his glory. All the nations will be gathered before him, and he will separate them one from another as a shepherd divides his sheep from the goats. He will put the sheep on his right and the goats on his left.

"Then the King will say to those on His right, 'Come, you who are blessed by my Father; take your inheritance, the kingdom prepared for you since the creation of the world. For I was hungry and you gave me something to eat, I was thirsty and you gave me something to drink, I was a stranger and you invited me in, I needed clothes and you clothed me, I was sick and you looked after me, I was in prison and you came to visit me.'

"Then the righteous will answer him, 'Lord, when did we see you hungry and feed you, or thirsty and give you something to drink? When did we see you a stranger and invite you in, or needing clothes and clothe you? When did we see you sick or in prison and go to visit you?'

"The King will reply, 'Truly I tell you, whatever you did for one of the least of these brothers and sisters of mine, you did for me'" (Matthew 25:31–40 NIV).

After listening to this beautiful soul share his greatest pain, the Holy Spirit in me proceeded to share hope through the saving message of Jesus Christ. I watched the Lord work through this unworthy vessel (me) to lead this beloved man in the salvation prayer and straight into the arms of the tenacious Lover, Jesus. When I walked away, I was humbled. I knew that my new brother in Christ was going to be okay. I watched his countenance go from depressed to delighted, from despair to joyfulness, from feeling lost to having purpose and hope.

Let me tell you, friends, that encounter changed me forever as I came to the realization that God had changed two lives that day. You see, even though I was a believer, I had failed to totally submit my time, focus, schedule, and fears of what-ifs to Him. I knew I was going to heaven because I had surrendered my life to Jesus, but I was missing "the rest of the story," as the late Paul Harvey would say. Jesus wanted all of me. It was that day that my precious Jesus showed me what the greatest commandment to love Him and love others (Mark 12:30–31) looked like, and when I chose to allow the Holy Spirit to have complete access, then and only then could I love Him and others tenaciously. This was my purpose, my calling.

He reminded me that I was His, a daughter of the King, and He wanted to set my agenda every day. My life was a platform to love tenaciously. This required me to filter people through the Holy Spirit so I could truly perceive and not just see. Seeing is really just observing a situation, we all do that, but perception is a true gift of the Holy Spirit and requires attention, awareness, and, a lot of times, engagement. Don't get me wrong, I am not saying jump out of the car every time you see someone in need, but what I encourage you to do is invite Jesus into every part of your day and ask the Holy Spirit to guide you to those places and people who need to hear from Him through you. These divine opportunities and detours come in all shapes and sizes, all ages, and in different environments. Every day is chock-full of these beautiful moments to love our Jesus tenaciously by loving those He puts in our path. This is once again where the rubber meets the road, friends. If we are all His, then it is no longer about us but about the One whom we represent.

Someone out there is feeling hopeless, invisible, and is praying for someone to see them. Will you allow the Holy Spirit to send you and be their answer to prayer? I encourage you to hand over your agenda and let the divine Scheduler schedule your next appointment.

Reflection:

Ask the Holy Spirit to reveal areas in your life that you are needing to surrender to Him. Remember, God has sent Him to help guide you and teach you all things (John 14:26), and He is faithful and will do it. Take this time to journal your prayer of surrender to Him and give Him full access to every moment of your day, week, and life. Ask Him to open your eyes so you can see the very ones around you that He has called you to reach out to. Put your seatbelt on, my friend, He is on the move!

- *Think about your day, week, month. What have you been about?*

- *What is your focus throughout the day? Are you focusing on your to-do list or leaving room for the Holy*

Spirit to bring divine opportunities through His divine detours in your day?

- *What encounters has the Lord placed in your path? Have you seen others who are outside of your schedule?*

- *What is keeping you from embracing the divine appointments God is placing in front of you?*

- *How would you feel if someone went out of their way to encourage you during a rough day?*

Journal: What will you choose?

Journal:

_____

_____

_____

_____

_____

_____

_____

_____

_____

_____

_____

TENACIOUS LOVE

CHAPTER TWELVE

Is Anything I Do Ever Good Enough?

"I can't seem to do anything right."

Ever feel this way? Wow, let me tell you, dear friend, I feel this way often, especially when I am around certain individuals who have the tendency to point out what they see as faults. You know those people who want you to do things their way? The micromanagers of society... It's amazing how often we as humans allow individuals such as these to steer our way of thinking, which, unfortunately, can lead us down a path of feeling inadequate. This can be a huge stumbling block. But God is always faithful to teach us something about ourselves and others through these encounters, *if* we choose to listen.

I will never forget the day I wanted to bless someone dear to me by making them breakfast. I was on an ATV trip with loved ones and it was a celebratory day, as it was a very special anniversary of a big accomplishment. To play it safe, I decided to make something simple in nature. You see, I thought I could make this person feel loved by serving them a meal and acknowledging their big day. What happened next will forever be ingrained in my memory...

I served what I believed was a nice meal, only to be hammered over the appearance of the bacon. I thought I was mentally prepared as I went into this, knowing that this individual was extremely picky and wanted every drop of fat off the bacon. So I crisped that bacon until it was almost unrecognizable, which is how they liked it. However, this is where it went extremely wrong. Wanting to bring some fun and humor into the meal, I crimped the bacon to make it look like a smile. Oh my stars! What transpired next was a barrage of negative comments over the appearance of the bacon that left me in the corner of the kitchen wiping away tears.

I ran into another room and grabbed my Tenacious Love journal and Bible. I was sure that the Lord was going to tell me, "Oh, Valerie! Wow, that took the cake, you really have every right to be angry and hurt! That bacon comment is unforgivable!"

But not surprisingly, what the Holy Spirit showed me was something very different. He called me to stop and evaluate the situation, my heart, and the person. Remember KYP—know your people? After the Lord helped me disembark from the emotional roller coaster, I realized, yes, I was hurt, but over bacon? Really? I was kicking myself, thinking how petty it was... "Get over it!" I tried to tell myself.

However, let's face it, when we've been offended, every emotion can either lead us to healing or to adding another brick to our wall. This person was a glass-half-empty kind of person, and I had always taken the critical comments and buried them deep in my heart, which was the problem. What the Holy Spirit revealed to me was that I allowed the enemy to try to open an old wound and use a familiar tactic of trying to make me feel that I am never going to be good enough. It brought back emotions from my childhood that if everything was not perfect, then I was a failure. The bacon was just the tipping point. However, God was so incredibly good and patient to use this petty encounter to remind me that this went much deeper than a piece of charcoaled meat. You see, this individual had experienced many situations throughout their life that left them feeling out of control. And they had just gone through a major medical journey and were still dealing with a lot of "uncontrollable" variables. So, if the bacon was something that could be controlled, then for the LOVE, *don't mess with the bacon!*

While my feelings were hurt by this individual's response to my attempt to bless them, taking them to the Lord and asking Him to show me what was truly behind it was a game changer for me. You see, my focus had been back on myself. *I* was just trying to bless this individual and impart something that *I* thought was fun! To be honest, had this incident happened before God gave me the tenacious love message, I would have let this "bacon encounter of 2019" be another brick in the wall between me and this person whom I love dearly. However, because God had been working on my heart, I was able to receive His message and ask Him what I was to do with the pain.

Let's face it, knowing the backstory of the offender doesn't always make the pain of the offense go away, especially when we are the repeated targets of their own pain. But in God's economy, every pain has a purpose. When it came down to it, it wasn't about bacon at all, it was about me doing something that was different, which left the other person feeling out of control. After all, don't we all do this from time to time? Especially when we use control and fault finding as a coping mechanism for our pain or insecurities?

Jesus experienced this on epic levels when He dealt with the Pharisees. He always saw the person and the need; they saw change and felt shamed by Jesus, resulting in their attempts to do anything to regain control, even if it meant "taking out the threat."

"When he had departed from there, He went into their synagogue. And behold, there was a man who had a withered hand. And they asked Him, asking, 'Is it lawful to heal on the Sabbath?'—so that they might accuse Him. Then He said to them, 'What man is there among you who has one sheep, and if it falls into a pit on the Sabbath, will not take hold of it and lift it out? Of how much more value then is a man than a sheep. Therefore it is lawful to do good on the Sabbath.' Then He said to the man, 'Stretch out your hand!' And he stretched it out, and it was restored as whole as the other. Then the Pharisees went out and plotted against Him, how they might destroy Him" (Matthew 12:9–14 NKJV).

Everything Jesus did was scrutinized and criticized by one or more of the Pharisees. They were control freaks and fault finders. Here Jesus was trying to teach them by showing them His tenacious love for humanity, but all they saw was change and rebellion. They took the bait of the enemy and missed the incredible blessing of seeing the Messiah and being transformed by His healing message. However, Jesus never let these people or their comments, glares, or plots against Him derail Him from persisting in His existence and fulfilling His divine purpose.

What God also put on my heart that day was how often I have been the offender. Let's be honest, it's easy to make a list of all those who have offended us by hurting our feelings in this area, but what about others' list of offenses? Are we on them? When I stop and consider how many times I have ramrodded others by thinking my way was the only way, my heart hurts. I have done this, and have been that person on so many occasions who has missed the blessing of others because I was so focused on the process...because of my insecurities. Can you imagine how different each of our lives would be if we chose to ask the Holy Spirit to help us perceive others through His perspective in this area? To see others' hearts and intentions towards us and realize that God has built them also with talents and giftedness. I believe we would all become champions of each other and learn to help one another through our insecurities. We truly would be able to "encourage one another daily, as long as it is called 'Today,' so that none of you may be hardened by sin's deceitfulness" (Hebrews 3:13 NIV).

At the end of the day, God showed me that every encounter has the ability to bring us closer to Himself and others, *if* we choose to invite Him into every hurt, offense, or difficult situation we have with other people. Our emotions matter to Him, even over something as trivial as bacon. While there are so many other larger offenses, the bacon incident was a catalyst that forced me to look deeper into the other individual's heart as well as my own. When God says He will use *all things* for the good, I can now add a crispy burnt bacon "smile" to the list!

Reflection:

- *Are you struggling with someone who is a fault finder in your life?*

- *Think about the individual's backstory and how that frames their perspective.*

- *Do you criticize others because you like things to be done "your way"?*

- *What is God calling you to do?*

Journal: What will you choose?

Journal:

_____
_____
_____
_____
_____
_____
_____
_____
_____
_____
_____
_____
_____
_____
_____
_____
_____
_____
_____

TENACIOUS LOVE

CHAPTER THIRTEEN

For the Love... Can't We Embrace Our Differences?

Are we attacking each other because we think differently? Why? Every day we watch the news and see the tensions rise throughout our cities, states, nation, and world. Why are we all turning on one another and allowing the enemy to establish factions even within our closest relationships? Why does one race, political party, or social class think they are better than another? Don't we all bleed the same? Haven't we all been made in the beautiful image of the Creator? Yes. The answer is *yes*. I believe we all can be a powerful force of unity, if we choose to allow the Holy Spirit to help us maneuver through these tumultuous waters of division and in the tenacious love of Christ.

I have mixed emotions when it comes to social media. I believe it can be a beautiful platform to connect with others, but outside the realm of kindness, respect, and love, it can be used as a tool of the enemy. From time to time I post things that I get excited about: prayer, family, friends, community unity, encouraging and inspirational stories, including decisions made by governing officials that honor and glorify God.

The other day I noticed a fellow Christian bashing me on my own page for posting something that they didn't like because they did not agree with me. This was an article that showed one governing official's stance on a Biblical principle. Yet this individual thought that their opinion, because they did not like the person, needed to be heard and proceeded to "voice" it on my page. I found myself baffled by their gumption to go on another's page and vent their venom against this official. You see, while I may not always agree with governing officials and their choices, I do believe that all authority is God-placed (Romans 13:1–6) and truly desire to honor God by praying for them, not attacking them. So, you can see why this individual's decision really chapped my khakis, resulting in my initial fleshly response of wanting to end my social media relationship with them. But God gently reminded me that tenacious love does not mean fleeing from those who think differently. In fact, we play right into the enemy's hands when we let these things divide us. What the enemy wants to use for evil, God will use for the good (Genesis 50:20) if we ask Him to instruct us on how He would like us to respond.

After my initial emotionally driven response I scrolled down on my social media page to find another comment that proved to be a powerful example of common ground and unity. Another friend posted, "I am not a fan of the person, but I can appreciate their stance." There it is, the solution. I think along the way we have been duped to believe that anyone who does not think the same way we do is against us and is an "enemy." We have put positions, politics, and policies over people. This is why I believe it is imperative to remember the enemy is the one casting the nets of division, yet there is always a hole in his net. It is called the truth and love.

Look at the world. We have become this side or that side and have let these differences build a wall of division to the extent that anyone who thinks differently is shunned for their beliefs, and dare I even say persecuted either verbally or through acts of violence. What do you think would happen if we found common ground somewhere and started building relationships on those very things? I have found, dear friends, that this is extremely difficult because it requires each of us to put our "right to be right" aside and ask the Holy Spirit to clothe us in humility, resulting in a "right to unite" focus, resulting in tenacious love. I am not saying compromise God's truth. That is where we stand fast. I am talking about petty differences that divide the body of Christ. Think about it, in Jesus' eyes we are all the same, no individual is better than another. That is why Jesus emphasized that we are all one in Him.

"So in Christ Jesus you are all children of God through faith, for all of you who were baptized into Christ have clothed yourselves with Christ. There is neither Jew or Gentile, neither slave or free, nor male or female, for you are all one in Christ Jesus" (Galatians 3:26–28 NIV).

I have found that in order for us to truly be united, God not only desires us to submit to Him, but He also calls us to forgive those who have offended us through these types of persecution. "Bear with each other and forgive one another if any of you has a grievance against someone. Forgive as the Lord forgave you. And over all these virtues put on love, which binds them all together in perfect unity" (Colossians 3:13–14 NIV).

Think about what would transpire if we all made an intentional decision to go directly to God in prayer, not passing through social media or collecting two hundred dollars' worth of others' opinions, and asked Him to help us respond in humility and find common ground with one another? What if we made a choice to see others as beautiful images of our Creator instead of rivals and "enemies" and chose to love each other tenaciously through our disagreements? What if we chose to see the person who is speaking out of their own experiences and actually took the time to invest in each one and hear their stories and begin a dialogue? What if?

I truly believe we can love tenaciously without having everything in common. However, in order to do that, it takes an intentional choice to submit to the Holy Spirit and ask Him to empower us to respond in His love. Remember, if He is in control then we will demonstrate the fruit of the Spirit (Galatians 5:22–23). Yet I have found this to be one of the most difficult things to do along this journey of tenacious love because we each are coming from our own experiences, and we can be passionate about our perspective. When we do not allow the other person to share their perspective then we lose the battle because we have lost the opportunity to validate a life...and the enemy wins, resulting in division, hurt, anger, etc. The truth is, we each have, through the power of the Holy Spirit, the ability to choose tenacious love and be the beautiful change we so desperately need.

We need a revival in our cities, states, nation, and world, but I believe the choice begins within each one of us. Think about the divisions in your life; what is holding you back from unity? Is it perhaps pride, stubbornness, or just flat-out rebellion? The beautiful truth is you still have breath in your body, you have the power of the Holy Spirit in you, and God is giving you another opportunity to be part of the healing process. What will you choose?

Reflection:

- *Do you have someone in your life that stirs you up every time you see them or hear their name?*

- *What is it about this person that has this effect on you?*

- *Ask the Holy Spirit to show you common ground that you can stand on with this person. What is He revealing?*

- *What is He telling you that you need to do to tenaciously love this person?*

- *Ask the Holy Spirit to reveal areas in your life that you are needing to surrender to Him.*

Journal: What will you choose?

Journal:

_____

_____

_____

_____

_____

_____

_____

_____

_____

CHAPTER FOURTEEN

Discarded

"I can't do this anymore. I feel like all I do is pour myself out, only to be used and discarded."

Ever feel this way? Have you ever given everything, only to be used and replaced, with not even a thank you or acknowledgment of your efforts? I have been on both sides of this. I have been discarded and, without meaning to, have done it to others. Let's face it, this hurts. What do we do with these emotions?

I had to learn the value of this lesson after working for the same employer for over twenty-one years. I had been a part of an amazing Christian organization from the beginning and was dear friends with the founders. As time passed, the founders began to retire and pass away, which opened up opportunities for others to step into leadership. This is where everything changed. You see, the founders loved Jesus tenaciously and made sacrifices, working tireless hours away from family, going without pay, and giving their everything to start the institution. They knew who they worked for and also knew it was only by the power of the Holy Spirit that the ministry would succeed. Jesus was the foundation and every decision was made through God's holy Word and prayer.

As new individuals came into the picture, the focus changed. The ministry aspect of the organization, where Jesus and people were the priority, now became motivated by numbers and cash flow. It became a dog-eat-dog business where everything and everyone was expendable. While I believe the leaders loved Jesus, I also believe they got ensnared by the enemy's trap to compete with other institutions. They had to be the best, and because of this perspective, they chose to strive and work harder to be number one rather than continuing to trust in the Lord's provision. I witnessed this and it was heartbreaking; these were my friends, my "family," so what did I do? I spoke up. I met with leadership and poured out my concerns, only to have them fall on deaf ears...ears that did not want to hear the truth. Friends, when God's Word gets watered down to accommodate another agenda, look for the enemy to be in the midst.

I will never forget the day God called me to move on. He knew that I had been struggling to remain there because of the changes, and He had been stirring my heart to support first responders by starting a nonprofit. When the day came for me to leave, I was treated as if I were just another replaceable part, leaving me feeling that the twenty-one years I poured out for the organization had been in vain. Let me tell you, this hurt did not go away overnight. I wrestled with God and could not let the pain go. It took me to a place that I had never been before.

Let's face it, dear friends, when we get emotionally run over by the very people we thought were in our corner, it leaves a mark that does not fade on its own. It takes our tenacious loving Savior to teach us how we are to respond. And this takes time. What God did over the next year was amazing. He saw me, He knew what I poured out, He saw me fight for truth and for others to be seen, and in His incredible economy, He used my gifts and experience to help the nonprofit take off in ways that I had never anticipated. He worked everything out for the good.

I believe living in such a fast-paced world fosters these types of encounters, and if we don't acknowledge the individuals whom God strategically places in front of us to help us along this journey called life, we can run over one another in the process of moving to the next thing. I am heartbroken to admit, I fear I have done this too many times in the past, and now I ask the Holy Spirit daily to help me see others from His divine perspective. I don't want anyone to feel as if they don't matter. I want everyone to know the tenacious love of God and that He sees everything that is poured out. Nothing is ever wasted in His economy, not even our greatest pains and failures.

He sees you, my friend.

I challenge you to stop and think about your life. How did you get here? How did you find yourself doing what you are now doing? When I stop and think about these very questions, I find myself overwhelmed by God's sovereignty and favor but also saddened by the fact that I have, from time to time, taken for granted the very ones who have encouraged me, prayed for me, and helped me along the way. In my drive to get to the next place, I fear I may have forgotten to acknowledge and honor precious people and my faithful, tenacious loving God along the way.

Jesus understood what it felt like. "Now on his way to Jerusalem, Jesus traveled along the border between Samaria and Galilee. As he was going into a village, ten men who had leprosy met him. They stood at a distance and called out in a loud voice, 'Jesus, Master, have pity on us!' When he saw them, he said, 'Go, show yourselves to the priests.' And as they went, they were cleansed. One of them, when he saw he was healed, came back, praising God in a loud voice. He threw himself at Jesus' feet and thanked him—and he was a Samaritan. Jesus asked, 'Were not all ten cleansed? Where are the other nine? Has no one returned to give praise to God except this foreigner?' Then he said to him, 'Rise and go; your faith has made you well'" (Luke 17:11–19 NIV).

The beautiful gift Jesus gives us in these Scriptures is that even though nine of the healed men did not acknowledge what Jesus did for them, one did. So how do we continue to pour ourselves out knowing that we may never be thanked or acknowledged? We live for *the One*. "Whatever you do, work at it with all your heart, as working for the Lord, not for human masters, since you know that you will receive an inheritance from the Lord as a reward. It is the Lord Christ you are serving" (Colossians 3:23–24 NIV).

And if we are all being honest with ourselves, we can also see that we have all been like the nine who were blessed and then ran off to the next thing, forgetting the very One who has changed our lives. I have done this, and if I am not intentional about going back to the One to thank Him and ask Him for His help to see others, then I can revert to the "me, myself, and I" world and disregard others and what they have done for me.

Like me, have you been so driven and self-focused that you have not acknowledged the tenacious loving One and the others He has put in your path to help you through this journey called life?

The beautiful thing is the One, Jesus, will never leave you and is walking through this journey with you. He will redeem lost opportunities as well as your pain of feeling discarded. You are the apple of His eye and He loves you tenaciously!

Reflection:

- *Ask God to reveal the people He has strategically placed throughout your life who have prayed for you, encouraged you, supported you, stood beside you, and loved you unconditionally.*

- *Have you acknowledged them by letting them know how instrumental they have been in your life? Explain.*

- *Ask the Holy Spirit to reveal anyone you are holding a grudge against because you have felt used or discarded by them. What is He revealing to you?*

- *What choices are you going to intentionally make in order to live for an audience of one?*

- *Ask the Holy Spirit to reveal areas in your life that you are needing to surrender to Him.*

Journal: What will you choose?

Journal:

_____
_____
_____
_____
_____
_____
_____
_____
_____
_____
_____
_____
_____
_____
_____
_____
_____
_____
_____
_____
_____
_____
_____
_____
_____
_____
_____
_____

TENACIOUS LOVE

CHAPTER FIFTEEN

Stop the World, I Want to Get Off!

"Oh my stars, another day of the same pressures and tensions. I am so exhausted; I don't think I can keep going!"

Have you ever felt this way? Oh, my friend, I have to tell you I am writing this from that very place. It seems as if I wake up each day to find the world worse off than the day before. It's as if it is spiraling downward at a rapid rate before my very eyes. There are angry words said here, violence there, and pain, hurt, and division everywhere. What has happened to the world I once knew? You know the one where people worked together and had each other's backs? The one that respected authority? The one where you could walk down the street without having to always look over your shoulder to make sure you were not in the crossfire of others' prejudices and disputes? You know that world? I am writing this amidst the COVID-19 pandemic and the George Floyd death at the hand of a police officer who misrepresented the badge. People are scared, they are angry, they want justice, they are protesting, they are looting, they are killing police, and then there is the social distancing and masks… It's like something out of a sci-fi novel.

While I understand there are things worth fighting for, like all people being treated with respect and equality, I also have come to know that some people just want to lie, kill, and destroy…just like the enemy. So how are we to tenaciously love in a world where there is so much hate and violence? How do we keep ourselves from being sucked into all the emotions that come with so much pain? How do we carry one another's burdens without carrying others' offenses? We know the answer: we keep our eyes fixed on Jesus and we hand over our emotions to the Holy Spirit and ask Him to use them for the good…to be counter cultural and for Him to love tenaciously through us.

Do you think Jesus went through the same social tensions and injustices? Do you think He stood up for what was right in God's eyes? You bet He did. Did He make a stand? Absolutely. "Jesus entered the temple courts and drove out all who were buying and selling there. He overturned the tables of the money changers and the benches of those selling doves. 'It is written,' he said to them, '"My house will be called a house of prayer," but you are making it "a den of robbers."' The blind and the lame came to him at the temple, and he healed them. But when the chief priests and the teachers of the law saw the wonderful things he did and the children shouting in the temple courts, 'Hosanna to the Son of David,' they were indignant" (Matthew 21:12–15 NIV).

I sometimes think we forget that anger is an emotion given to us, but we must be very intentional to not let this emotion take us from righteous anger to unrighteous action. Jesus made a stand. Do you think He was angry? He turned over tables and called out the ones who had perverted the temple. However, what did He do after that? Did He go on destroying the town? Verbally bashing those who were selling in the temple? No, He made His statement, and then He continued to live a life that reflected tenacious love. He loved His heavenly Father so much that He felt the need to make a stand against the straight-up defilement of His house.

I think so often we feel we are not meant to stand up and say something when people defile our God and do things to put money, power, greed, pride on the throne, resulting in others being used and mistreated. However, I am here to tell you, as my personal opinion, that is not true. What's my foundation for making this statement? Scripture is chock-full of people whom God called and empowered to take a stand, including Noah, Abraham, Moses, Esther, Daniel, Peter, Paul, and so many others who act as incredible examples for each of us. Jesus Himself called out the Pharisees for that very thing. Thinking they were better and misusing and abusing those who were beneath them, they thought that money, power, education, and social status made them superior… but Jesus called them out.

So what can we learn from Jesus' example in order to love tenaciously in a world that is not at all different from the world Jesus lived in?

We can continue to be intentional about looking to Jesus as our example, surrendering our feelings and emotions to the Holy Spirit and allowing Him to empower us to tenaciously love the offenders. "For this reason I kneel before the Father, from whom every family in heaven and on earth derives its name. I pray that out of his glorious riches he may strengthen you with power through his Spirit in your inner being, so that Christ may dwell in your hearts through faith. And I pray that you, *being rooted and established in love*, may have power, together with all the Lord's holy people, to grasp how wide and long and high and deep is the love of Christ, and to know this love that surpasses knowledge—that you may be filled to the measure of all the fullness of God. Now to him who is able to do immeasurably more than all we ask or imagine, according to his power that is at work within us, to him be glory in the church and in Christ Jesus throughout all generations, for ever and ever! Amen" (Ephesians 3:14–21 NIV, emphasis added).

After all, each one of us is undeserving of His tenacious love, yet it is freely given. If we are being completely honest, each one of us has been on the other side where we have offended.

So I challenge you, the next time you feel angry at what is happening around you, ask yourself these questions:

Am I offended personally or is this an offense against our heavenly Father? If it is personal, we must learn to hand it over to God. If the offense is against our heavenly Father and everything He stands for, then we must make a stand. However, it is imperative that we get the truth from His Word and humble ourselves before the Holy Spirit, ask Him to direct our path, and allow Him to lead.

It was once said, "Do not pray for easy lives; pray to be stronger people! Do not pray for tasks equal to your powers; pray for powers equal to your tasks."

Reflection:

Ask the Holy Spirit to give you a discerning spirit and reveal areas in your life where you are harvesting anger that you need to surrender to Him. What is He telling you?

- *Ask God to reveal the people you are struggling with.*

- *What is it about these individuals that has you struggling?*

- *Ask the Holy Spirit to reveal the root of the struggle.*

- *What Scripture verses address the "root" and will help guide you in the truth?*

Journal: What will you choose?

Journal:

_____
_____
_____
_____
_____
_____
_____
_____
_____
_____
_____
_____
_____
_____
_____
_____
_____
_____
_____
_____

_____
_____
_____
_____
_____
_____
_____
_____
_____
_____
_____
_____
_____
_____
_____
_____
_____
_____
_____
_____
_____
_____
_____
_____
_____
_____

Phillips Brooks, Leadership, Vol 6, no.3 "Do not pray for easy lives; pray to be stronger people! Do not pray for tasks equal to your powers; pray for powers equal to your tasks."

CHAPTER SIXTEEN

Does My Life Even Matter?

Ever feel like you are in the movie *Groundhog Day*? You know, where you wake up each day to find the same needs, demands, and responsibilities waiting for you? "Oh, my stars, didn't I *just* do this yesterday *AND* the day before?" I don't know about you, but feeling this way makes me want to bury my head in my pillow and push the SNOOZE button, hoping the responsibilities will somehow fade away. However, I have found life, and all it brings, whether good or bad, will always be there waiting for us. What I have found makes the difference is where we get our strength and perspective.

I remember feeling this way on a daily basis while raising my children. My husband would get up every morning and head to work while I was home with my cherubs. Don't get me wrong, I loved being home with them and felt as if God had given me an incredible gift by allowing me to do so. However, it was a season that required sacrifice, structure, discipline, and the same routine day in and day out in order to help give my children a sense of security. This type of daily routine can leave one feeling invisible and exhausted and asking, Does this matter? Do I matter?

For you it may not come in the form of raising children but perhaps in a job, tending to a sick or elderly loved one, or perhaps even in a marriage. But Jesus shows us that everything we do matters to God. Think about Him and His life. We read in the Synoptic Gospels (Matthew, Mark, Luke, and John) how Jesus continued to persist in His existence. Day in and day out He got up and was inundated with the same needs of others, physical, spiritual, and emotional. Yet He knew that behind every need was a soul and behind every encounter was a divine opportunity. We must remember that in Jesus' humanity, these encounters must have left Him physically and emotionally exhausted. But what did He do?

"It happened when He was in a certain city, that behold, a man who was full of leprosy saw Jesus; and he fell on his face and implored Him, saying, 'Lord, if You are willing, You can make me clean.' Then He stretched out His hand and touched him, saying, 'I am willing; be cleansed.' Immediately the leprosy left him. And He charged him to tell no one, 'But go and show yourself to the priest, and make an offering for your cleansing, as a testimony to them, just as Moses commanded.' However, the report went around concerning Him all the more; and great multitudes came together to hear, and to be healed by Him of their infirmities. *So He Himself often withdrew into the wilderness and prayed*" (Luke 5:12–16 NKJV, emphasis added).

Throughout the Gospels we see that Jesus often withdrew Himself from people and all the demands, and sought solitude with His Father. Why? Because of the intimate relationship He had with His Father. We also see Jesus having the strength to continue in His journey after spending time with His Father in prayer.

I have come to realize that I too *need* to have time with my heavenly Father in order to be refilled, empowered, and directed for my next steps. I have come to greatly appreciate the beauty in God's design for relationship. He desires to commune with each one of His children. Yes, this means you as well, my friend!

So, when we feel the demands of each day, let us withdraw in solitude and ask the very One who created us to bathe us in His tenacious love and encourage and teach us to persist in our existence, even if it feels like what we are doing is small and unnoticed.

Reflection:

- *Ask God to reveal what you are struggling with.*

- *Why do you feel you are struggling in this area?*

- *Ask the Holy Spirit to reveal the root of the struggle.*

Journal: What are you going to do?

Journal:

_____
_____
_____
_____
_____
_____
_____
_____

DOES MY LIFE EVEN MATTER?

CHAPTER SEVENTEEN

Tenacious Love...Is It Worth It?

This is too hard... I am not changing anything... I can't do this anymore... Is this even worth it?

If you, like me, have been intentionally choosing to surrender to the Holy Spirit and ask Him to help you to love tenaciously, then I'm sure these thoughts and questions have been a constant in your journey. And like me, you have come to realize this journey is far from easy; in fact, it is most difficult. It is the narrow road, the road less traveled, and I daresay some days you even feel as if the narrow road is a tightrope. It is lonely, discouraging, painful, sacrificial, full of ups and downs, but I can say with full confidence it is worth it! Remember every encounter is an opportunity to glorify our heavenly Father and to be salt and light in this world.

"You are the salt of the earth; but if the salt loses its flavor, how shall it be seasoned? It is then good for nothing but to be thrown out and trampled underfoot by men. You are the light of the world. A city that is set on a hill cannot be hidden. Nor do they light a lamp and put it under a basket, but on a lampstand, and it gives light to all who are in the house. Let your light so shine before men, that they may see your good works and glorify your Father in heaven" (Matthew 5:13–16 NKJV).

As you have embraced this lifetime journey of intentionally loving others through Jesus' example and through the power of the Holy Spirit, know *you* are positively impacting our world and are a beautiful representation of our Savior Jesus Christ. You, my friend, are a world changer! We have come to realize through this journey that offenses come in small and large encounters, and we as humans have been the offenders as well as the recipients. However, we have also come to realize every intentional choice to surrender our emotions to the Holy Spirit and allow Him to love others tenaciously through us, even when flesh and all its emotions want to do the opposite, leads us to a stronger and more intimate relationship with our God, and prepares us for the next encounter.

As Jesus resolutely set out on His journey to the cross to show each one of us what the perfect example of tenacious love looks like, we too are each on our individual journey. This is not a one-and-done type of study. It is a lifetime, heart-changing, intentional journey with our Savior. I know each one of you will have your own stories that will encourage those around you and bring God glory. I am so proud of you. Thank you for joining me on this journey. Together, with the power of the Holy Spirit and through Jesus' example, we shall choose to love tenaciously.

Reflection:

- *Go back to your first several journal entries and read what the Holy Spirit has taught you.*

- *How has your heart changed?*

- *Ask the Holy Spirit to bring to memory your greatest victories.*

- *Ask the Holy Spirit to search your heart and reveal areas that are still needing to be surrendered to Him.*

Journal your prayer of thanksgiving and continued surrender to Him on your final journal page.

Journal:

_____

_____

_____

_____

_____

_____

_____

_____

_____

_____

_____

_____

_____

_____

_____

_____

_____

CONCLUSION

In the beginning of this book I mentioned my friend Sherry, whose choice to love the offender tenaciously in the courtroom impacted lives on epic levels. However, the story did not end there. During the process of writing this book God did something beyond measure. Several months ago Sherry received a call notifying her that the woman who hit and killed her husband had given her life to Christ! Sherry was so moved that she contacted the church this young lady attended to set up a meeting with her...and she asked me to join them. I was overwhelmed that my friend would invite me to be part of such a holy moment, and I eagerly responded with a resounding yes.

The day of the meeting came. Sherry and I, along with Sherry's sister Lynne, were in the parking lot praising God for what He had done and praying for what was to come. As we walked inside the church we were greeted by the most beautiful woman. I mean this woman was radiant and the Lord shone around her. To my surprise, it was Miranda, the offender! I didn't even recognize her. The last time I had seen her was in the courtroom, and let me tell you it was evident that she was a new creation! Then, in what I can only describe as a miraculous moment, she and Sherry embraced.

This embrace was a beautiful sign of a new beginning, one that moved me to tears.

What is God doing? I asked myself, and I could not wait to see what was next! After spending a couple hours sitting with Miranda and Sherry, it became evident that God had moved mountains in both lives to bring us to this moment. You see, while Sherry continued to tenaciously love Miranda by praying for her for ten years, God was changing Miranda's heart. I felt beyond privileged to be able to hear about the total transformative work God did to bring Miranda to this place. She had not only surrendered her life to Jesus, but He was now using her to minister to young ladies within the same juvenile system that she experienced! Now that's the power of our God! Only He can do something like this. It reminded me that nobody is beyond His reach and that His arm is never too short to save anybody (Isaiah 59:1).

Sherry and Miranda now meet often over God's Word. They are actively involved in each other's lives and are sharing their story of God's redemptive power. What I have learned through being an eyewitness of this incredible miracle is that God honors choice, and because of His tenacious love for us, He is always working for the good. Sherry will be the first to tell you that God prepared her years before through small choices to love tenaciously, even in the midst of pain and loss. This inspires me, and I hope you, to keep choosing love, knowing that God never sleeps and is working in ways that are beyond anything we can hope or imagine.

I wholeheartedly desire to choose to live out the remainder of my days loving Him and others tenaciously. How about you?

Do you have a tenacious love story that you would like to share?

Contact Valerie Jameson at
tenaciouslovestory@gmail.com

All Scripture references are from:

- The Holy Bible, New International Version (NIV) Zondervan Bible Publishers.

- The New King James (NKJV), Thomas Nelson, Inc.

WHAT THE BIBLE SAYS
ABOUT TENACIOUS LOVE

"A new commandment I give to you, that you *love* one another; as I have loved you, that you also *love* one another." John 13:34–35 NKJV (emphasis added)

Therefore, if you have any encouragement from being united with Christ, if any comfort from his love, if any common sharing in the Spirit, if any tenderness and compassion, then make my joy complete by being like-minded, having the same love, being one in spirit and of one mind. Do nothing out of selfish ambition or vain conceit. Rather, in humility value others above yourselves, not looking to your own interests but each of you to the interests of others. In your relationship with one another, have the same mindset as Jesus Christ, who, being in very nature God, did not consider equality with God something to be used to his own advantage; rather, he *made himself* nothing by taking the very nature of a servant, being made in human likeness. And being found in appearance as a man, he humbled himself by becoming obedient to death—even death on a cross! Therefore God exalted him to the highest place and gave him the name that is above every name, that at the name of Jesus every knee should bow, in heaven and on earth and under the earth, and every tongue acknowledge that Jesus Christ *is Lord*, to the glory of God the Father. Philippians 2:1–11 NIV (emphasis added)

God so loved the world that He gave His only begotten Son, that whoever believes in Him should not perish but have everlasting life. John 3:16 NKJV

When the teachers of the law who were Pharisees saw him eating with the tax collectors and sinners, they asked his disciples: "Why does he eat with tax collectors and sinners?" On hearing this, Jesus said to them, "It is not the healthy who need a doctor, but the sick. I have not come to call the righteous, but sinners." Mark 2:16–17 NIV

If you declare with your mouth, "Jesus is Lord," and believe in your heart that God raised Him from the dead, you will be saved. For it is with your heart that you believe and are justified, and it is with your mouth that you profess your faith and are saved. Romans 10:9–10 NIV

Submit yourselves, then, to God. Resist the devil, and he will flee from you. Come near to God and He will come near to you. James 4:7–8 NIV

Each tree is recognized by its own fruit. People do not pick figs from thornbushes, or grapes from briers. A good man brings good things out of the good stored up in his heart, and an evil man brings evil things out of the evil stored up in his heart. For the mouth speaks what the heart is full of. Luke 6:44–45 NIV

Since, then, you have been raised with Christ, *set* your hearts on things above, where Christ is seated at the right hand of

God. Set your minds on things above, not on earthly things. For you died, and your life is now hidden with Christ in God. When Christ, who is your life, appears, then you also will appear with him in glory. Put to death, therefore, whatever belongs to our earthly nature: sexual immorality, impurity, lust, evil desires and greed, which is idolatry. Because of these, the wrath of God is coming. You used to walk in these ways, in the life you once lived. *But now* you must also *rid* yourselves of all such things as these: anger, rage, malice, slander, and filthy language from your lips. Do not lie to each other, since you have taken off your old self with its practices and have put on the new self, which is being renewed in knowledge in the *image* of its Creator. Colossians 3:1–10 NIV (emphasis added)

Whatever is true, whatever is noble, whatever is right, whatever is pure, whatever is lovely, whatever is admirable—if anything is excellent or praiseworthy—think about such things. Philippians 4:8 NIV

For though we walk in the flesh, we do not war after the flesh. For the weapons of our warfare are not carnal but mighty through God for pulling down strongholds, casting down arguments and every high thing that exalts itself against the knowledge of God, bringing every thought into captivity to the obedience of Christ. 2 Corinthians 10:3–5 NKJV

Those who live according to the flesh have their minds set on what the flesh desires; but those who live in accordance with the Spirit have their minds set on what the Spirit desires. The mind governed by the flesh is death, but the mind governed by the Spirit is life and peace. The mind governed by the flesh is hostile to God; it does not submit to God's law, nor can it do so. Those who are in the realm of the flesh cannot please God. You, however, are not in the realm of the flesh but are in the realm of the Spirit, if indeed the Spirit of God lives in you. Romans 8:5–13 NIV

The acts of the flesh are obvious: sexual immorality, impurity and debauchery; idolatry and witchcraft; hatred, discord, jealousy, fits of rage, selfish ambition, dissections, factions and envy; drunkenness, orgies and the like... But the fruit of the Spirit is *love*, joy, peace, forbearance, kindness, goodness, faithfulness, gentleness and self-control. Galatians 5:19–23 NIV (emphasis added)

Therefore be imitators of God as dear children. And walk in love, as Christ also has loved us and given Himself for us, an offering and a sacrifice to God for a sweet-smelling aroma. Ephesians 5:1–2 NKJV

Let us make mankind in *our* image, in our likeness, so that they may rule over the fish in the sea and the birds in the sky, over the livestock and all the wild animals, and over all the creatures that move along the ground. Genesis 1:26 NIV (emphasis added)

See, I set before you today life and prosperity, death and destruction. For I command you today to love the LORD your God, to walk in obedience to him, and to keep his commands, decrees and laws; then you will live and increase, and the LORD your God will bless you in the land you are entering to possess. Deuteronomy 30:15–16 NIV

But to you who are listening I say: *Love* your enemies, *do good* to those who hate you, *bless* those who curse you, *pray for* those who mistreat you. If someone slaps you on one cheek, turn to them the other also. If someone takes your coat, do not withhold your shirt from them. Give to everyone who asks you, and if anyone takes what belongs to you, do not demand it back. *Do to others as you would have them do to you.* If you love those who love you, what credit is that to you? Even sinners love those who love them. And if you do good to those who are good to you, what credit is that to you? Even sinners do that. And if you lend to those from whom you expect repayment, what credit is that to you? Even sinners lend to sinners, expecting to be repaid in full. But *love* your enemies, *do good* to them, and *lend* to them without expecting to get anything back. Then your reward will be great, and you will be children of the Most High, because he is kind to the ungrateful and wicked. *Be merciful,* just as your Father is merciful. Luke 6:27–36 NIV (emphasis added)

And we know that in *all things God works for the good* of those who love him, who have been called according to his purpose. Romans 8:28 NIV (emphasis added)

Praise be to the God and Father of our Lord Jesus Christ, the Father of compassion and the God of all comfort, who comforts us in all our troubles, so that we can comfort those in any trouble with the comfort we ourselves receive from God. 2 Corinthians 1:3–4 NIV

But God demonstrates His own love toward us, in that while we were still sinners, Christ died for us. Romans 5:8 NKJV

For it is by grace that you have been saved, through faith— and this is not from yourselves, it is the gift of God—not by works, so that no one can boast. Ephesians 2:8 NIV

Now the serpent was more crafty than any of the wild animals the LORD God had made. He said to the woman, "Did God really say, 'You must not eat from any tree in the garden'?"

The woman said to the serpent, "We may eat fruit from the trees in the garden, but God did say, 'You must not eat fruit from the tree that is in the middle of the garden, and you must not touch it, or you will die.'"

"You will not certainly die," the serpent said to the woman. "For God knows that when you eat from it your eyes will be opened, and you will be like God, knowing good and evil."

When the woman saw that the fruit of the tree was good for food and pleasing to the eye, and also desirable for gaining wisdom, she took some and ate it. She also gave some to her husband, who was with her, and he ate it. Then the eyes of both of them were opened, and they realized they were naked; so they sewed fig leaves together and made coverings for themselves.

Then the man and his wife heard the sound of the LORD God as he was walking in the garden in the cool of the day, and they hid from the LORD God among the trees of the garden. But the LORD God called to the man, "Where are you?"

He answered, "I heard you in the garden, and I was afraid because I was naked; so I hid."

And he said, "Who told you that you were naked? Have you eaten from the tree that I commanded you not to eat from?"

The man said, "The woman you put here with me—she gave me some fruit from the tree, and I ate it."

Then the LORD God said to the woman, "What is this you have done?"

The woman said, "The serpent deceived me, and I ate."
Genesis 3:1–13 NIV

For God hath not given us the spirit of fear; but of power, and of love, and of a sound mind. 2 Timothy 1:7

When Jesus had said these things, He was troubled in spirit, and testified and said, "Most assuredly, I say to you, one of you will betray Me." John 13:21 NKJV

Jesus answered, "Those who have had a bath need only to wash their feet; their whole body is clean. And you are clean, though not every one of you." For he knew who was going to betray him, and that was why he said not everyone was clean.

When he had finished washing their feet, he put on his clothes and returned to his place. "Do you understand what I have done for you?" he asked them. "You call me 'Teacher' and 'Lord,' and rightly so, for that is what I am. Now that I, your Lord and Teacher, have washed your feet, you also should wash one another's feet. I have set you an example that you should do as I have done for you. Very truly I tell you, no servant is greater than his master, nor is a messenger greater than the one who sent him. Now that you know these things, you will be blessed if you do them. John 13:10–17 NIV

"My grace is sufficient for you, for my power is made perfect in weakness." Therefore I will boast all the more gladly about my weaknesses, so that Christ's power may rest on me. That is why, for Christ's sake, I delight in weaknesses, in insults, in hardships, in persecutions, in difficulties. For when I am weak, then I am strong. 2 Corinthians 12:9–10

He entered the synagogue again, and a man was there who had a withered hand. So they watched Him closely, whether He would heal him on the Sabbath, so that they might accuse

Him. And He said to the man who had the withered hand, "Step forward." Then He said to them, "Is it lawful on the Sabbath to do good or to do evil, to save life or to kill?" But they kept silent. And when He had looked around at them with anger, being grieved by the hardness of their hearts, He said to the man, "Stretch out your hand." And he stretched it out, and his hand was restored as whole as the other. Then the Pharisees went out and immediately plotted with the Herodians against Him, how they might destroy Him. Mark 3:1–6 NKJV

He came to His own, and His own did not receive Him. John 1:11 NKJV

When the Son of Man comes in His glory, and all the holy angels with Him, then He will sit on the throne of His glory. All the nations will be gathered before Him, and He will separate them one from another, as a shepherd divides his sheep from the goats. And He will set the sheep on His right hand, but the goats on the left. Then the King will say to those on His right hand, "Come, you blessed of My Father, inherit the kingdom prepared for you from the foundation of the world: for I was hungry and you gave Me food; I was thirsty and you gave Me drink; I was a stranger and you took Me in; I was naked and you clothed Me; I was sick and you visited Me; I was in prison and you came to Me."

Then the righteous will answer Him, saying, "Lord, when did we see You hungry and feed You, or thirsty and give You drink? When did we see You a stranger and take You in, or naked and clothe You? Or when did we see You sick, or in prison, and come to You?"

And the King will answer and say to them, "Assuredly, I say to you, inasmuch as you did it to one of the least of these My brethren, you did it to Me." Matthew 25:31–40 NKJV

Now when He had departed from there, He went into their synagogue. And behold, there was a man who had a withered hand. And they asked Him, saying, "Is it lawful to heal on the Sabbath?"—that they might accuse Him.

Then He said to them, "What man is there among you who has one sheep, and if it falls into a pit on the Sabbath, will not lay hold of it and lift it out? Of how much more value then is a man than a sheep? Therefore it is lawful to do good on the Sabbath."

Then He said to the man, "Stretch out your hand." And he stretched it out, and it was restored as whole as the other. Then the Pharisees went out and plotted against Him, how they might destroy Him. Matthew 12:9–14 NKJV

Encourage one another daily, as long as it is called "Today," so that none of you may be hardened by sin's deceitfulness. Hebrews 3:13 NIV

So in Christ Jesus you are all children of God through faith, for all of you who were baptized into Christ have clothed yourselves with Christ. There is neither Jew or Gentile, neither slave or free, nor male or female, for you are all one in Christ Jesus. Galatians 3:26–28 NIV

Bear with each other and forgive one another if any of you has a grievance against someone. Forgive as the Lord forgave you. And over all these virtues put on love, which binds them all together in perfect unity. Colossians 3:13–14 NIV

Now on his way to Jerusalem, Jesus traveled along the border between Samaria and Galilee. As he was going into a village, ten men who had leprosy met him. They stood at a distance and called out in a loud voice, "Jesus, Master, have pity on us!"

When he saw them, he said, "Go, show yourselves to the priests."

And as they went, they were cleansed. One of them, when he saw he was healed, came back, praising God in a loud voice. He threw himself at Jesus' feet and thanked him—and he was a Samaritan.

Jesus asked, "Were not all ten cleansed? Where are the other nine? Has no one returned to give praise to God except this foreigner?" Then he said to him, "Rise and go; your faith has made you well." Luke 17:11–19

Whatever you do, work at it with all your heart, as working for the Lord, not for human masters, since you know that you will receive an inheritance from the Lord as a reward. It is the Lord Christ you are serving. Colossians 3:23–24

Jesus entered the temple courts and drove out all who were buying and selling there. He overturned the tables of the money changers and the benches of those selling doves.

"It is written," he said to them, "'My house will be called a house of prayer,' but you are making it 'a den of robbers.'"

The blind and the lame came to him at the temple, and he healed them. But when the chief priests and the teachers of the law saw the wonderful things he did and the children shouting in the temple courts, "Hosanna to the Son of David," they were indignant. Matthew 21:12–15 NIV

For this reason I kneel before the Father, from whom every family in heaven and on earth derives its name. I pray that out of his glorious riches he may strengthen you with power through his Spirit in your inner being, so that Christ may dwell in your hearts through faith. And I pray that you, *being rooted and established in love,* may have power, together with all the Lord's holy people, to grasp how wide and long and high and deep is the love of Christ, and to know this love that surpasses knowledge—that you may be filled to the measure of all the fullness of God. Now to him who is able to do immeasurably more than all we ask or imagine, according to his power that is at work within us, to him be glory in the church and in Christ Jesus throughout all generations, for ever and ever! Amen. Ephesians 3:14–21 NIV (emphasis added)

It happened when He was in a certain city, that behold, a man who was full of leprosy saw Jesus; and he fell on his face and implored Him, saying, "Lord, if You are willing, You can make me clean."

Then He put out His hand and touched him, saying, "I am willing; be cleansed."

Immediately the leprosy left him. And He charged him to tell no one, "But go and show yourself to the priest, and make an offering for your cleansing, as a testimony to them, just as Moses commanded."

However, the report went around concerning Him all the more; and great multitudes came together to hear, and to be healed by Him of their infirmities. *So He Himself **often** withdrew into the wilderness and prayed.* Luke 5:12–16 NKJV (emphasis added)

You are the salt of the earth; but if the salt loses its flavor, how shall it be seasoned? It is then good for nothing but to be thrown out and trampled underfoot by men. You are the light of the world. A city that is set on a hill cannot be hidden. Nor do they light a lamp and put it under a basket, but on a lampstand, and it gives light to all who are in the house. Let your light so shine before men, that they may see your good works and glorify your Father in heaven. Matthew 5:13–16 NKJV

ACKNOWLEDGMENTS

We are not meant to do this life alone, and this book is a perfect example of that very statement. First and foremost, I must acknowledge the Holy Spirit for giving me the life-changing message of tenacious love and the words to write this book. Without Him I would not have had the courage to step out in faith.

I am incredibly blessed with a strong community of supporters, from my precious family members to friends I call family, who have each prayed for me and encouraged me to step out of my comfort zone and share this journey. Thank you, I love each of you.

I would also like to thank every individual that has crossed my path throughout my life. Whether it was a brief and casual encounter or a longer relational investment, either way you have impacted my life in ways you may never know. Perhaps you invited me to go in front of you while changing lanes on the road, or served me a meal at a restaurant, or checked out my groceries at the store and asked how my day was going, or even offered me a warm smile while handing me my coffee from a drive-through window. Or perhaps you coached with me, taught with me, mentored me, prayed with me, were in my classroom, played on my team, lived in my neighborhood, served with me at my church, or protected and served my community... Know you have played a tremendous part in this tenacious love journey and I will forever be grateful for the gift of each of you.

Keep loving and seeing others. You are changing the world!

ABOUT THE AUTHOR

Valerie Jameson is a New Mexico native who has spent her life investing in people. She considers herself abundantly blessed to be the wife of her tenacious-loving husband, Kevin, for thirty-three years, a mother of two faithful and adored sons, a mother-in-law to her two beautiful and compassionate daughters-in-law, a grandmother to two vivacious and tender-hearted grandsons, a daughter to a wise and sacrificial mother and father, a sister to three incredible life-giving siblings, a daughter and sister-in law to kind and hard-working in-laws, and friend to a multitude of beautiful and diverse people across the globe.

Valerie holds degrees in advertising and public relations and is an ordained senior chaplain. She is also the founder of Stand True, Inc. a nonprofit that supports first responders and their families. Valerie believes every life has a powerful purpose and that every intentional choice to see and love God and others can impact the world on epic levels.